Fascin

Facts, Mysteries & Myths

About U.S. Coins

Robert R. Van Ryzin

©2009 Krause Publications, Inc., a subsidiary of F+W Media, Inc.

Published by

krause publications
A subsidiary of F+W Media, Inc.

700 East State Street • Iola, WI 54990-0001
715-445-2214 • 888-457-2873
www.krausebooks.com

Library of Congress Control Number: 2009925863

ISBN-13: 978-1-4402-0650-4
ISBN-10: 1-4402-0650-3

Designed by: Paul Birling
Written by: Robert R. Van Ryzin

Printed in
United States of America

*A*s this book is a compilation of research over the years, there are plenty of people who have influenced its creation, even if not directly involved in its production. Some of them are mentioned here.

Although I did set aside some coins as a child, I didn't become a collector until 1976. I bought a copy of *Coins* magazine at a local grocery store and have been hooked ever since.

In the 1980s I went back to school to obtain my master of fine arts degree in history. There, I was fortunate enough to have professors who allowed me to write course papers dedicated to different aspects of U.S. currency history. It was there that I came to know and admire Dr. Watson Parker, who has a number of books to his credit, including seminal research into the history of Deadwood, S.D., and the Black Hills, and who encouraged me (and other students) to submit works for publication.

I still remember many of the pieces of advice Parker gave concerning research and writing. I hope that I have a least partially lived up to his dedication and expertise in these regards.

I'm also thankful to all of those currently in the numismatics division here at Krause Publications and those who have served in those functions in years past. Though there have been many changes, with people coming and going, I've appreciated their encouragement and their dedication to this hobby. Thanks particularly to Chet Krause and Cliff Mishler for their early and continued hobby leadership and foresight and for supporting my earlier books.

For the current effort in producing this book, I'm especially thankful to graphic artist Paul Birling for his work on its layout, which has greatly helped to bring the stories within to life. Thanks also to my wife Sharon, a gifted writer in her own right, who assisted with proofreading the text and offered valuable suggestions.

Robert R. Van Ryzin
August 2009

Fascinating Facts, Mysteries & Myths
About U.S. Coins

★ ★ ★

★★★

*R*ecently a wild turkey flew into the tree behind our house. It stayed only a short time before it continued on its way, but it reminded me of Ben Franklin and the CBS television show "WKRP in Cincinnati" (1978-1982).

Why Franklin? Because he is remembered by coin collectors for his objection to using the depiction of an eagle as a national symbol. In a January 1784 letter from France to his daughter Sally, Franklin complained that the bald eagle in the Great Seal adopted by the Congress in 1782 looked more like a turkey than an eagle. "For my own part," he wrote, "I wish the Bald Eagle had not been chosen the Representative of our Country. He is a Bird of bad moral Character." The turkey, he said, was a "much more respectable Bird"... "He is besides, though a little vain & silly, a Bird of Courage."

So, if Franklin had had his way, Tom Turkey would now be on all of our coins, and not just our dinner tables.

Why "WKRP in Cincinnati"? Well, many readers will remember the episode titled "Turkeys Away" from the 1978 season and written by Bill Dial, in which Arthur Carlson (Gordon Jump), the station's general manager, decides as a WKRP promotion for Thanksgiving to drop 20 live turkeys from a helicopter on holiday shoppers below. Carlson, who wouldn't tell the staff what the promotion was, assured them it was going to be "one of the greatest events in gobbler history."

News director Les Nessman (Richard Sanders) reported the scene live as some of the birds came plummeting to the ground. When he realized what was dropping from the helicopter, Nessman exclaimed, "Oh, the humanity!... The turkeys are hitting the ground like sacks of wet cement!... Not since the *Hindenburg* tragedy has there been anything like this!"

Carlson later explained, "As God is my witness, I thought turkeys could fly."

The turkey in my backyard, however, didn't have much trouble flying onto a tree branch some 15 feet off the ground.

★★*

Another reason this episode of "WKRP in Cincinnati" came to mind was that in doing research for this book, I came across reference to the television show in the pages of *Numismatic News*. In 1980, the American Numismatic Association's annual convention was held in Cincinnati, and the *News* reported that three actors from WKRP were also members of the ANA and collected coins. These included Richard Sanders, Frank Bonner (who played salesman Herb Tarlek) and Tim Reid (Venus Flytrap).

It was a reminder that there are some great stories and interesting people related to this hobby. Even prior to joining the editorial staff of Krause Publications late in 1986, I always found the story behind the coin to be the most fascinating part of the hobby.

My first article published in a major hobby tabloid concerned such a story—the tale of Ezra Meeker and his attempts to mark the Oregon Trail, which as a young man he had traveled as part of the great westward migration following the discovery of gold in California. You'll find details of his efforts within.

Since then, I've done considerable research into the models for the Indian Head nickel, the real story behind the design change on the Standing Liberty quarter, and the myths that have grown up over the years concerning various coins and their designs. You'll also find research about the model for the Saint-Gaudens gold $20 and the still-controversial claim by sculptor Dr. Selma Burke's that she should have been credited for the design on the Roosevelt dime.

Scattered through the main chapters, you'll also come across interesting tidbits culled from hobby publications, including the more than half century of issues of *Numismatic News*. I hope you enjoy them.

Robert R. Van Ryzin

★ ★ ★

Isaac Johnny John (John Big Tree) was a bit actor in many early westerns. He even appeared in a silent film in the late 1920s shot at Glacier National Park at about the time Two Guns White Calf, who was a star attraction there, was touring the United States as a model for the Indian Head nickel.

★★★

Chapter 1

Mistaken Identity

Here's a story that's been told and retold to the point where just about every time a collector picks up a magazine or book, it's somehow gone askew.

The story is that Two Moons, a Cheyenne; Iron Tail, a Sioux; and a third Indian, whose name sculptor James Earle Fraser couldn't remember, served as models for the Indian Head nickel (1913-1938).

Unfortunately, Fraser's faulty memory, along with the coin's lifelike depiction of a noble American Indian, left the door ajar for several missing "third" models to step through. One of

The design on James Earle Fraser's Indian Head nickel (1913-1938) was meant to typify America.

★ ★ ★

those who eagerly entered and has since taken up permanent residence in the hearts and minds of collectors is Isaac Johnny John, a Seneca of the eastern Iroquois Nation, better known as Chief John Big Tree.

The tale of how he mistakenly came to be accepted as a model for Fraser's work is a fascinating one — wedded to the romance of the Old West, to the desperate plight of the American Indian, to attempts by whites to capitalize on the nation's seemingly unquenchable thirst for fanciful stories of an untamed past, and to artists who sought to capture the American Indian's image and spirit on canvas and in magnificent, powerful, and often poignant sculptures.

Against this backdrop, splattered with the paint of a thousand tall tales, John Big Tree applied his own colorful, if less than truthful, brush, claiming to have been the model for the forehead and the nose of the design. Aided by a great sense of the theatrical, perfected over years of work in Hollywood (including appearances in such early screen epics as John Ford's "The Iron Horse" and "Drums Along the Mohawk") and early 1960s promotional appearances across the nation, he was able to falsely taint the history of this coin's artistic origins.

Today, through the help of numismatic writers, he has risen to almost folklore status within the hobby and remains the most mentioned "third" model for Fraser's coin. Forgotten are the glaring inconsistencies in his story that led some writers of his day to dismiss him as a fraud. Overlooked are scattered references to a different "Big Tree," this one a Kiowa, Adoeette, whom evidence suggests is a more likely candidate. Remembered and recounted instead is the old chief's spoon-fed cock-and-bull story that he posed for the nose and forehead of the Indian Head nickel, while a Sioux (Iron Tail)

James Earle Fraser credited his interest in the American Indian to his upbringing in South Dakota.

★★★

modeled for the cheek and chin of the likeness and a Cheyenne (Two Moons) for the hair and headdress.

Toward a new design

The story of how Chief John Big Tree came to his lofty status begins in 1911, when Fraser responded to Treasury Secretary Franklin MacVeagh's call for a new design to replace the Liberty Head nickel.

Two Guns White Calf, also known as John Two Guns or Whitecalf Two Guns, was perhaps the most photographed Indian of his day.

★ ★ ★

Two Guns White Calf sports a medallion with the Buffalo nickel design. He likely came to honestly believe he was a model for the coin, despite Fraser's denial.

Fraser had already gained international acclaim for his stirring depiction of a trail-bitten, downtrodden Indian in his *End of the Trail* statue. He had also endeared himself with President Theodore Roosevelt through sculpting a much-acclaimed bust of the president. The two became fast friends, with Fraser a natural selection as part of Roosevelt's drive to upgrade the nation's coinage.

The new coin, bearing its realistic representation of an American Indian on the obverse and a bison on the reverse, was released into circulation in 1913. Shortly thereafter the Treasury Department was inundated with letters from the public hoping to learn the identity of the Indian on the new nickel. Unfortunately, Fraser had trouble remembering the names of his models. The question would be broached so many times that many of his responses, each structured in a slightly different manner, appear to reflect his increasing disinterest and distaste for the topic, rather than a true attempt to set the record straight.

An undated (circa 1913) letter to Mint Director George E. Roberts suggests that Fraser considered the Indian design represented a type, rather than a direct portrait. The question of the models was apparently of secondary importance to the artist.

He said he could recall Two Moons, a Cheyenne, and Iron Tail, a Sioux, as having served as the inspiration. Also, possibly, "one or two others." In later years he dropped the number of possible other models to one, and at times shrugged off such inquiries, directing his secretary to provide the stock answer.[1]

The initial press coverage on the new coin was also unclear. An article by D.H. De Shon, of the Utica, N.Y., *Herald-Dispatch*, reprinted in the May 1913 issue of *The Numismatist*, erroneously proclaimed the design showed an "artistically executed head of a

★★★

Comanche Indian."[2] The March issue of *The Numismatist* more correctly reported that it was based on a Cheyenne who visited Fraser in New York.[3]

Kodak snap-shootin'

One Indian not mentioned by Fraser, who quickly captured public attention and acceptance as one of the models, was Chief Two Guns White Calf, a Blackfoot. Two Guns' claim lost a great deal of validity, however, when in 1931, Fraser vigorously denied having used him as a model.

JOSH'S GOLDEN RACKET

Soon after the release of the Liberty Head nickel, in 1883, rumors began to circulate that the coins, which displayed the "V" for "five cents" on the reverse without the addition of word "cents," would be recalled. It was also reported that the coins were being plated and passed off as $5 gold coins.

According to numismatic lore, the leader among all these petty crooks was Josh Tatum, a deaf-mute from Boston who took $50 worth of the new coins to a Boston pawnbroker, who owned a gold-plating machine, to be plated. Tatum then set out to spend one of his new "gold" coins at a tobacco store, where he purchased a five-cent cigar by laying the coin on the counter and receiving $4.95 in change.

He repeated this process at various tobacco stores, disposing of the entire 1,000 coins within a week.

Tatum and the jeweler decided to plate 5,000 more and took their scam on the road between Boston and New York, dumping about 2,000 more before authorities caught up with them.

At his trial, the defense presented by Tatum's lawyer was simple: Josh never asked for change.

The case being dismissed, the government moved to stop any further abuse by placing the word "cents" on the coin.

The lack of the word "cents" on the first Liberty Head nickels led some to gold plate the coins and try to pass them as $5 gold pieces.

* ★ *

A copy of a June 10, 1931, letter from Fraser to the Commissioner of Indian Affairs of the U.S. Department of the Interior (released to the press on July 12, 1931) quotes Fraser as saying:

HAPPY MOTORING

To assist the war effort, the Mint changed from a copper composition for the cent to a zinc-coated steel version for one year, in 1943. A few examples are known to have escaped the Mint struck on copper planchets.

Rumors circulated in the 1940s that the Ford Motor Co. would give a car to anyone finding a 1943 copper cent. It wasn't true, but it probably led to the creation of additional bogus copper-plated cents of that year.

In 1943 the cent was minted in zinc-coated steel (as is this specimen). However, a few examples escaped the Mint on copper planchets.

The Indian head on the Buffalo nickel is not a direct portrait of any particular Indian, but was made from several portrait busts which I did of Indians. As a matter of fact, I used three different heads; I remember two of the men. One was Irontail, the best Indian head I can remember; the other one was Two Moons, and the third I cannot recall.

I have never seen Two Guns Whitecalf nor used him in any way, although he has a magnificent head. I can easily understand how he was mistaken in thinking that he posed for me. A great many artists have modeled and drawn him, and it was only natural for him to believe that one of them was the designer of the nickel. I think he is undoubtedly honestly of the opinion that his portrait is on the nickel.

I am particularly interested in Indian affairs, having as a boy lived in South Dakota before the Indians were so carefully guarded in their agencies. Later, the Crow Creek agency was formed at Chamberlain, but I always feel that I have seen the Indian in his natural habitat, with his finest costumes being worn. I hope their affairs are progressing favorably.[4]

★★★

One of the few bronzed originals of James Earle Fraser's *End of the Trail* statue can be found in Waupun, Wis.

A clue to how Two Guns White Calf became convinced that his likeness was used on the nickel and how the legend continued to flourish, despite Fraser's denial, comes from an article by syndicated columnist Elmo Scott Watson published in various newspapers in 1938, as the Indian Head nickel was being supplanted by the new Jefferson type.[5]

Watson wrote that Two Guns bore such a striking resemblance to the Indian on the nickel that many who visited the chief at Montana's Glacier National Park thought they were viewing the coin's model. So did the Indian, who Watson says, honestly believed the coin was designed after his likeness.

"So the legend persisted," Watson wrote, "and when the Blackfoot died in 1934, the familiar story (with pictures, of course) blossomed out in full flower again, thus proving that error, as well as truth, when 'crushed to earth will rise again.'"

* ★ *

GOLD SACAGAWEAS

The Sacagawea dollars are golden in color, but they're not minted in gold—at least not all of them. A dozen 2000-W Sacagawea proof dollars were minted in .9167-fine gold, in a slightly larger size than the circulation versions, and flown on Space Shuttle *Columbia's* July 1999 mission, which was commanded by Eileen Collins, the first female commander of a shuttle flight. The coins were created for promotional reasons and as patterns for possible collector versions of the design. The space-flown coins were on display at the American Numismatic Association's "World's Fair of Money" in Milwaukee in 2007.

Watson said it was hard to trace the origin of the story, but provided the following, given to him by Hoke Smith, Western development agent of the Great Northern Railroad:

> You asked for it, I consulted the sages of the tribe, and here is the real story of the Indian face upon the nickel, as near as I can translate it from the Blackfoot spoken and sign language:
>
> Many moons ago, when he was in his early thirties, the late Chief Two Guns White Calf, chief of the Glacier National Park Blackfoot tribe, got his first nickel from one of the earlier spendthrift tourists that came to his tepee, kodak snap-shootin'. It was one of the buffalo series of five-cent pieces.
>
> Two Guns was delighted with the picture of the Buffalo, which side happened to be 'tails up' when the generous tourist put it in the palm of his hand. A moment later, when he turned the coin over and beheld his own likeness standing in bold relief before him, it was as lookin' into a mirror to Two Guns.
>
> 'Me!' he exclaimed. 'Big White Chief put warrior on penny. But when it come to nickel only chief is big enough.' It happened the 'liberal-handed' tourist Two Guns was talking to was a news photographer 'grabbing some photo feature' stuff while visiting the park. Straightaway he went out and seized the buffalo nickel Indian feature and gave it wide circulation.

* ★ *

While Two Guns White Calf lived (for twenty years after) he was hailed by every school child in the United States as the Indian whose face appeared on the buffalo nickel. And there was much controversy throughout the land![6]

Murky waters

One of the first numismatic writers to wade into the murky waters surrounding the design controversy was Marianne F. Miller. Her article, "Buffaloed by the Buffalo Nickel," in the October 1956 issue of *Numismatic Scrapbook Magazine,* lent wishful support to Two Guns White Calf as the missing model, while at the same time offhandedly dismissed Chief John Big Tree as a possible candidate.

Miller said her search for the identity of the third Indian was sparked by an item appearing in the September 1955 issue of *Numismatic Scrapbook Magazine,* which told of the arrest of Chief John Big Tree, 79, in Syracuse, N.Y., for driving while intoxicated. The notice said the Indian claimed to be one of the models for the Indian Head nickel.

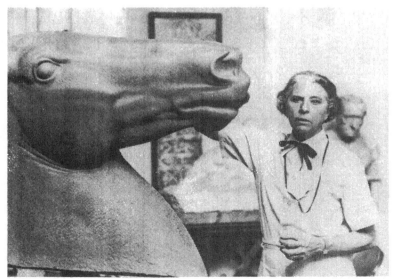

Laura Gardin Fraser, a sculptor and coin designer in her own right, ended up adding to the confusion over the third model for her husband's nickel design.

* ★ *

Miller set out to contact John Big Tree, but found him "not in the least cooperative." She added that she found "no other evidence to substantiate his claim."[7]

Miller said that after visiting the Treasury Department, the Bureau of Indian Affairs and the National Archives, over an 11-month period, along with writing 39 letters in an attempt to determine the name of the third model, she was sure of only one thing, "the buffalo nickel really had me buffaloed."

As part of her presentation, Miller argued that the U.S. Mint would not have allowed Fraser to directly portray any living person on the coin, implying that his statement about using a composite portrait may have been purposely aimed at disguising Two Guns' role in the design. It would also justify the artist's denial of ever using Two Guns as a model.

Her article is largely devoted to quotes from people who knew Two Guns, most of whom believed he was the model. Forrest R. Stone, superintendent of the Flathead Indian Agency in Dixon, Mont., who was with Two Guns when he died, told Miller he believed Two Guns' story; Frank Sherburne, who had lived on the Blackfoot reservation since 1896 and was well acquainted with Two Guns, expressed his belief that Two Guns was the model; and Waldon S. Arnholt, an artist from Ashland,

Chief John Big Tree became a regular on the show circuit. Here he is at the Texas Numismatic Association convention in 1966.

★

Versions of the Indian Head nickel were well underway before John Big Tree claimed to have modeled for the coin.

Ohio, who had used Two Guns as a model, was positive the portrait on the nickel was of Two Guns, right down to the eyes, ears, nose and mouth.

But when Frank Sherburne questioned Two Guns as to whether or not he was the model, Miller says, the chief admitted he did not know.

A lot of people had painted him, Two Guns apparently confided to Sherburne, but Two Guns said he kept his braids better than those on the coin, and when he wore a feather "it pointed up from the back of his head and not down like a whipped bird!"[8]

On request, Two Guns would also sign Indian Head nickels (for a premium) with his mark — two crossed rifles for the coins and two rifles and a young calf on pictures. He would even furnish the nickel.[9]

Enter stage right

Irked by Miller's story, Leonard J. Ratzman entered the fray in "The Buffalo Nickel, A 50-Year-Old Mystery," appearing in two parts in the May and June 1964 issues of the *Whitman Coin Journal.* Ratzman wrote:

> In every source of reference researched by this writer and others attempting to solve the same problem, it is agreed that the Cheyenne Two Moons and the Sioux Chief Iron Tail are definitely two of the three Indians used as models by Fraser. The identity

★★★

A wooden nickel produced to mark Chief John Big Tree's visit to Galveston, Texas, on March 26, 1966. The visit was sponsored by Falstaff Breweries.

of the third, however, has still not been identified after a half a century and has eluded every effort to be found.[10]

Citing Fraser's denial, Ratzman came to the conclusion Two Guns White Calf was not the model. Ratzman based his conclusion primarily on a July 1931 issue of the American Numismatic Association's journal, *The Numismatist*, which reprinted a widely circulated Associated Press dispatch, noting:

> That is not the face of Chief Two Guns Whitecalf on the Buffalo nickel. It is three other fellows, says an Associated Press dispatch.
>
> Ever since the present 5-cent piece was designed, about eighteen years ago, there have been stories to the effect that Two Guns was the original of the Indian head. Recently James E. Frazer [sic], who designed the coin, wrote the Indian Office that he had never seen Two Guns, but had used three different Indians to obtain the design. One was named Irontail, another Two Moons, a Cheyenne chief who is now dead. Frazer [sic] has forgotten the name of the other. Nevertheless Chief Two Guns has a magnificent head and many artists have modeled it.[11]

To prove that Chief John Big Tree deserved the honor, Ratzman said a meeting he had with the Indian in September 1962 was the "first in a long line of events that have lead to what is felt to be the solving of the identity of the third Indian."[12]

★★

At the time, John Big Tree was being billed as one of the main attractions of the Eastern States Exposition in Springfield, Mass. According to Ratzman, advance publicity for the event named John Big Tree, 97, as a model for the Indian Head nickel and provided biographical information.

Ratzman said John Big Tree was born near the end of the Civil War, "the son of helmsman aboard a Great Lakes steamer." By the time he was 14, John Big Tree had been bitten by the acting bug. He began to travel, moving from town to town by Indian wagon caravan, performing in nightly stands. The chief would later spend 35 years in Hollywood as an actor.

Given his chance to meet with John Big Tree, something Miller had found impossible, Ratzman inexplicably opted not to ask the chief if he had posed for the nickel.

"After meeting the Chief, this writer did not want to run into the same brick wall that Miss Miller did, so no attempt was made at the time to verify his claim," Ratzman wrote.[13] It was only after months of correspondence with the chief's publicity agent that Ratzman said a breakthrough came. The agent suggested he contact Dr. E.A. Bates, "an expert in Indian lore," who at one time worked in the Agriculture Department of Cornell University.

Bates' reply to Ratzman, dated June 24, 1963, tells of a meeting Bates claimed he had with Le Roy Fess, a feature writer for the *Buffalo News*. Though no date is given for the meeting, if it occurred, it must have taken place sometime prior to the nickel's release.

Bates told Ratzman that he had been in New York to give a speech when he met Fess. Fess, in turn, told Bates that he saw Fraser "pick up Big Tree while the Indian was modeling for a class in the Buffalo Art Museum." Bates wrote:

> That night, I saw John [Big Tree] on the Tonawanda (Seneca) reservation and I said, 'Well, John, I hear (from Fess) you are going to be on a coin.' He said no, but the drawer (artist) only wanted his nose. John's wife, Cynthia, said I should cut off some of John's nose, he's always in other people's business. One time at the Indian Village, a little while later, a man gave John a dollar for a photo and John said, 'That's more than I got for the Nickel.'[14]

* ★ *

Ratzman believed his search was over. For that matter, so did many numismatists.

Aided by Ratzman's bold article — published only a few months prior to a *Coin World* reprint of an article that identified the Kiowa Adoeette (Big Tree) as the third model — Chief John Big Tree was catapulted to the forefront.[15]

Don Taxay, in his 1966 book, *The U.S. Mint and Coinage: An Illustrated History From 1776 to the Present*, was caught up in the belief that Chief John Big Tree was the third model and referred to Ratzman's article as the source. Other writers since have

Adoeette, "Big Tree."

Courtesy National Archives.

variously named "Chief John Tree," "Big Tree," "Chief John Big Tree" or, sometimes, "John Big Tree, Kiowa," but generally intending reference to the Seneca/Iroquois Indian, not the Kiowa, Adoeette.

The belief that John Big Tree worked as a model for Fraser was amplified by the Indian's own efforts and the public's willingness to embrace him as a living symbol of America. The old Indian was regularly depicted in a nostalgic, Old West fashion — next to a tepee, standing with a bison or in full headdress.

When he visited Wisconsin in 1964 to help celebrate the city of Waupun's 125th anniversary, he graciously posed with a symbolic outstretched arm before a rare bronze original of Fraser's *End of the Trail* statue, located in the city's cemetery.

During that same period he made a guest appearance on the popular television show "What's My Line," where he successfully stumped a panel of celebrities. His line was that he posed for the nose and forehead of the famous coin.

★★★

For the cover photo of the March 1964 issue of *Esquire,* John Big Tree showed up at the magazine's studio wearing a business suit, overcoat and sporting a crew cut.

He told author Alice Glaser that he posed for the nickel in 1917 and received his first nickel the following year.[16] Glaser corrected his dates, stating that Fraser had seen the chief working in a Wild West show on Coney Island in the summer of 1912 and had asked him to pose for the nickel. John Big Tree, she said, resisted, wanting to wait until the show season was over.

> **FS FOR SCHLAG**
>
> Although the first Jefferson nickel was released in 1938, designer Felix Schlag's "FS" initials didn't appear on the coin he designed until 1966, some 28 years later.

He began posing, she said, in November of that year and continued working for the artist through April of the following year — arriving at the artist's studio in the morning to model for the nickel and in the afternoon for the painting [sic, sculpture?] *End of the Trail.*

Unfortunately for the would-be model, first examples of the new coin entered circulation in February 1913, a month prior to the end of his supposed six-month stint as a model and long after initial plaster models had been prepared. Also, it's doubtful a skilled artist would have needed six months of the Indian's time to capture the look of his forehead and nose.

John Big Tree, it should be remembered, was an actor. He regularly played roles as Great Plains Indians in Hollywood. His appearance at *Esquire* was likely no different, just another acting job.

The record of John Big Tree's visit to the magazine's studio lends considerable insight into how a bit of makeup, an appropriate wig, and proper feathers could help convince the public that the illusion before them was real.

Makeover miracles

Glaser had written that when 87-year-old Isaac Johnny John entered Carl Fischer's studio for the photograph that would eventually grace the magazine's cover, the Indian was wearing a business suit and overcoat, with his hair in a crew cut. With a bit of help, an hour later he emerged from a dressing room dutifully made up in a black wig, makeup and wearing buckskin trousers.

* ★ *

A makeup artist then applied color to the chief's skin, explaining that "People expect red Indians to look red," and stuffed cotton wadding in the chief's mouth to fill the void where teeth used to be. This done, the illusion was completed. With an Indian Head nickel as a model, black and white feathers were positioned in the Indian's wig. A cut-up red bandana wrapped his newly made braids.[17]

PROTECTED FROM WEAR

Dates and denominations wearing off of coins has always been a problem for the U.S. Mint and for coinage designers. This was the case with the Standing Liberty quarter (1916-1930). Disappearing dates led to recessed dates from 1925 on.

A similar problem, but this time with the denomination, resulted in a quick alteration of the Buffalo nickel (1913-1938). The first issues, in 1913, showed the bison standing on a mound (Variety 1). This was, however, quickly changed that year to a design with the bison standing on a line (Variety 2). This was done to protect the denomination from wear.

First examples of the Indian Head nickel (Variety 1) showed the bison on the coin's reverse standing on a mound. Because of wear to the denomination, the Variety 2 1913 coins have the bison standing on a line.

★★★

Chief John Big Tree was thereby made to resemble the nickel — so much so that upon seeing a copy of the magazine cover, the artist's wife Laura Gardin Fraser is said to have identified him as a model for her husband's coin.

Writers Annette R. Cohen and Ray M. Druley, in *The Buffalo Nickel,* quote an April 17, 1964, letter from Laura Gardin Fraser to the Mint director. In it, she says, "the name of Big Tree always came to my mind" in relation to the third model for the Indian Head nickel, but that she wasn't certain until she saw the *Esquire* cover, sent to her on the occasion of the chief's 100th birthday.[18] Mrs. Fraser added that it was amazing that the chief had changed so little over the years. Surprisingly, she said she had never seen Iron Tail or Two Moons, this because she wasn't at the studio much during the time the coin was being modeled. The Frasers weren't married until 1913, after the nickel was released.

Frankly, at 100, or even 87 as the *Esquire* article notes, it's just not possible that John Big Tree hadn't changed much in appearance since 1911, when the first plaster models are believed to have been made. The cover photo depicts an aged Indian, something John Big Tree was not in 1911.

Of significance also is that Mrs. Fraser admitted only that she remembered an Indian named Big Tree. Seven years earlier she told a similar story of an Indian named Big Tree, identified by the author of that article as a Kiowa, Adoeette, whose anglicized name was Big Tree.[19]

Noting that "the controversy made for a crowded warpath," Norman Davis in his 1971 book, *The Complete Book of United States Coin Collecting,* wrote that "Chief John Big Tree (Seneca) believed for over 50 years that the coin showed him; when he died, newspapers honored his claim — until they began hearing from collectors who pointed out that he had no proof of the claim."[20]

If there was an outcry from collectors, as Davis suggested, it doesn't seem to have carried much weight in the long run, as today it has largely disappeared from the numismatic landscape.

One numismatic writer, who long ago questioned Chief John Big Tree's inability to remember his age, was Lee Martin. In his 1966 book, *Coin Columns,* Martin said that, after being arrested for drunken driving in 1955, Chief John Big Tree gave his age as 79; seven years later he was claiming to be 92; two years

★★★

MAKE IT IN SACAGAWEAS

Being paid for your work is one thing. Being paid for your work in the coins you designed is another. When sculptor Glenna Goodacre created the obverse design for the Sacagawea mini-dollar, released in 2000, she was paid $5,000 in Sacagawea dollars. However, these were slightly different than the Sacagaweas found in circulation in that they were burnished and treated with an antioxidant before being sealed in plastic tubes for delivery to Goodacre's studio in Santa Fe, N.M.

The coin's obverse was modeled by Randy'L He-dow Teton, a 24-year-old bachelor of fine arts graduate of the University of New Mexico in Albuquerque, who Goodacre said "shared facial characteristics of a Shoshone woman and served as an excellent model." Teton is a member of the Shoshone-Bannock/Cree Tribe of the Cree Nation.

Glenna Goodacre, designer of the Sacagawea mini-dollar, took her payment in 5,000 of the golden-colored coins.

after that he was 97. In 1966, one year before his death, he was 102. (At a Texas Numismatic Association convention that same year he told *Numismatic News* he was 104.)

"Evidently arithmetic was not his forte," Martin wrote, adding that if Chief John Big Tree was 79 in 1955, he would have been about 36 in 1912 when the coin was being modeled. Iron Tail and Two Moons were much older. Martin argued that it seemed questionable "that a skilled sculptor would have used one subject so different from the other portions in a composition. If, however, he truly is 101 years old today, then the story becomes more likely."[21]

Years later, writer Clement Bailey took a similar tack, observing that John Big Tree had learned his story well but had adopted "new math" before it was invented.

★★★

Unfortunately for John Big Tree, after his death on July 6, 1967, records kept by the Onondaga Historical Association showed him to be only 92 years old, meaning he was 36 in 1911 when the plasters of the Indian Head nickel were completed. By contrast, Iron Tail was 61 and Two Moons was 64. Adoeette was 64.

Iron Tail, a Sioux, was one of the American Indians Fraser used in designing the obverse of the new nickel.

An Associated Press obituary notice, datelined on the day of his death, told that the chief's Christian name was Isaac Johnny John and that he had played more than 100 minor parts in early Western movies, often describing himself as the "best bareback rider in Hollywood." Further, Isaac Johnny John claimed to have been born in 1862 "and sometimes showed an Indian head penny of that year, which he said was given to him by his grandfather as proof" of his age.

Reporting on Chief John Big Tree's attendance at the 1966 Texas Numismatic Association convention in Galveston, where the chief signed and gave away wooden nickels as part of a promotion for Falstaff Breweries, the April 25, 1966, issue of *Numismatic News* said:

> Chief John Big Tree, who claims to be 104 years old, is a full blooded Iroquois who now lives with his wife on the Onondaga Reservation near Syracuse, New York. He was one of three Indians selected to pose for the design of the buffalo nickel in 1912. The coin shows a buffalo on the reverse and an Indian on the obverse.
>
> According to the Chief, he was used as the model for the nose and forehead of the Indian nickel while a Sioux modeled for the cheek and chin of the likeness and a Cheyenne for the hair and headdress.

★ ★ ★

The idea of the portrait on the nickel was to represent the typical American Indian which resulted in three different tribes being used as models.

Chief Big Tree says he was working in a Coney Island show when he was chosen to pose, 'because of his classic facial features.'

He says he also posed for the famous art work, 'The End Of The Trail,' at the same time he was posing for the U.S. coin. He posed for the picture in the mornings and the coin in the afternoons.

Questions have been raised regarding the Indian's age, but Chief John Big Tree says he has an Indian head cent dated 1862 which his grandfather gave him at the end of the Civil War and told him 'never to part with the coin as it was struck in the year of Chief Big Tree's birth.'

The Chief claims to still have the cent, which in his opinion, is proof of the year in which he was born.[22]

Simple logic also brings John Big Tree's claim into doubt. Fraser grew up in South Dakota, where, he said, he counted Indians of several tribes, including the Dakotas, Sioux and Kiowa, as his friends. Several writers have recorded that his files were filled with photographs of Great Plains Indians. It's not likely that he needed to, or would have, relied on the features of an Indian from an Eastern tribe when there were so many plains Indians from which to choose. Although the design may have been a composite, it was, in Fraser's own words, intended to reflect the Indians of the Great Plains.

New York bound

The truth as to who, if anyone, was the missing third model most likely lies in a quote found in Dean Krakel's 1973 book *End of the Trail: Odyssey of a Statue.*

Through Fraser's unpublished memoirs, interviews with Laura Gardin Fraser and a host of other sources, Krakel thoroughly documented the careers of James Earle Fraser and Laura Gardin Fraser, while detailing his own efforts as director of the National Cowboy Hall of Fame to transfer and restore one of the remaining full-size *End of the Trail* statues.

★★★

COIN POUCHES

The 2004 Lewis and Clark Expedition commemorative silver dollar program offered an interesting option that included hand-produced pouches to go with a commemorative dollar. The U.S. Mint worked with the Circle of Tribal Advisors to obtain up to 50,000 pouches to accompany a coin-and-pouch offering. Each pouch came with a certificate of authenticity signed by the Native American who crafted it. The 11 tribal nations included descendants of the many American Indians encountered by Meriwether Lewis and William Clark.

In reference to the coin, he quotes Fraser as saying:

> In designing it, my objective was to achieve a coin which would be truly America, that could not be confused with currency of any other country. I made sure, therefore, to use none of the attributes which other nations had in the past. And in my search for symbols, I found no motif within the boundaries of the United States so distinctive as the American buffalo, or bison. The great herds of buffalo that roamed the Western plains played an important epic in winning the West.
>
> With the Indian head on the obverse, we have perfect unity in theme. It has pertinent historical significance, and is in line with the best traditions of coin design, where the purpose was to memorialize a nation or a people.[23]

Krakel adds that the Treasury Department received hundreds of letters asking the identity of the Indian model for the coin. Fraser, he said, wrote:

> In fact, the profile is a composite of three plains Indians — a Sioux, a Kiowa, and a Cheyenne. The three Indians were Iron Tail, a Sioux; Big Tree, a Kiowa; and Two Moons, a Cheyenne. The Indians had come to visit President Roosevelt and stopped off in New York. During this time, I was able to study and photograph them. The three had combined features of the hardy, virile types of Great Plains Indian.[24]

* ★ *

Unfortunately, Krakel misattributed this quote, the proceeding one, and one concerning the bison, Black Diamond, to Watson's article from the *Oceana Herald*. The correct attribution has not been located.[25]

The same quotes appear in William Bridges' 1974 work *Gathering of Animals: An Unconventional History of the New York Zoological Society* but without reference to source.

The misattributed bison quote, which by tone appears to be from the same source as Fraser's comments about the Indians, has been reproduced elsewhere and matches similar statements by Fraser.[26]

Any such visit by these Indians to New York would likely have occurred between 1901 and 1909, while Roosevelt was still in office. We know from Fraser's background that he was well acquainted with Roosevelt, having been recommended by Augustus Saint-Gaudens (for whom he was then serving as a studio assistant) to take on one of Saint-Gaudens' commissions — a bust of the president from life.

Fraser and Roosevelt shared a common interest in the West. It's not unlikely, therefore, that Roosevelt, aware of Fraser's interest in studying Indians, sent Two Moons, Big Tree and Iron Tail to see him. A suggestive reference by editor Edgar Adams in the March 1913 issue of *The Numismatist* seems to lend some credence, though no positive proof. Adams related:

> It is said that Mr. Fraser (the designer) took as a model an Indian of the Cheyenne tribe, who recently visited New York City.[27]

Two Moons is known to have traveled to Washington, D.C., and New York on a number of occasions. In fact, in February 1913, just after the nickel's release, the *New York Times* listed him among 30 or more chiefs visiting New York, including Sioux and Kiowa, for the dedication of a monument to the American Indian. Iron Tail, who traveled in a number of the famous Wild West shows, was also a frequent visitor to the East.

The positive identification of the Kiowa Adoeette as the model would certainly help to explain the confusion that has plagued numismatic writers since the early 1970s and 1980s. It's not at all unusual to find a writer name John Big Tree as the model, only to then show a National Archives' photograph of Adoeette; or identify John Big Tree as a Kiowa, not a Seneca.

* * *

An act of war

Is it possible Adoeette modeled? It certainly isn't without reason. Adoeette was a well known Kiowa chief and likely made visits to the East, as many in his tribe did.

He was also much more famous in his day than John Big Tree — his fame coming not from movie roles but from his real-life actions.

In 1871, Adoeette, along with Kiowa Chief White Bear, was convicted of first-degree murder and sentenced to die by hanging for his part in a gruesome raid on an Army supply train heading for Fort Richardson, Texas. Seven men were killed. The Indians, under White Bear's leadership, mutilated the living and the dead.

One teamster was found chained to his wagon, his tongue cut out; the teamster was burned to death.

Following their arrest and conviction, the fates of Adoeette and White Bear became the focus of humanitarian groups in the East, hoping to stay their execution. Even the Indian Bureau claimed that they had committed an act of war, not murder.

White Bear (top) and Adoeette were both convicted of first-degree murder and scheduled to hang.

The judge presiding at their trial wrote to Texas Gov. Edmund Davis suggesting a change in the sentence to life imprisonment at hard labor.

Public pressure finally led to their conditional release in 1873. The Indians were warned not to leave the reservation or they would go back to prison.

They did leave, however, and were again arrested in 1874. Adoeette and White Bear were taken to Fort Sill, Okla., where Adoeette was imprisoned and held until the following year. White Bear was sent back to Texas to serve a life sentence.

Adoeette later converted to Christianity and spent 30 years as a deacon for the Rainy Mountain Indian Mission. He died at Fort Sill on Nov. 13, 1929.

One biographer said, "He became a model of peaceful serenity in his old age." It is also most likely he became a model for a famous U.S. coin now incorrectly attributed to an Indian with the same name.

* ★ *

★★★

Chapter 2

Buffaloed

*A*ll right. So there is serious disagreement as to which Indians modeled for the obverse of James Earle Fraser's Indian Head nickel, but what about the bison on the reverse — is it Black Diamond? Well, despite the best intentions of numismatists to get this story straight, it's just about as twisted as any in the fable-strewn numismatic stable.

Fine specimen?

First, who was Black Diamond? By some accounts he was the finest specimen of a bison in captivity. By others, he was a mangy, droopy-headed, suicide-prone animal who made a timely trip to the dinner table as a high-priced steak.

Depending on which account you read, he was housed either at the Central Park Corral, Garden City Zoological Gardens, the Bronx Zoological Park, the New York Central Zoo, the Central Park Corral or the Bronx Park Zoo.

Unfortunately, as with the story of the models for the Indian on the obverse, the artist hasn't been much help. Fraser said of the animal:

★★★

He was not a plains buffalo, but none other than Black Diamond, the contrariest animal in the Bronx Park. I stood for hours watching and catching his form and mood in plastic clay. Black Diamond was less conscious of the honor being conferred on him than of the annoyance which he suffered from insistent gazing upon him. He refused point blank to permit me to get side views of him, and stubbornly showed his front face most of the time.[1]

Fraser's reference to a Bronx Park Zoo would cause confusion for some time to come. Add to that the Jan. 27, 1913, issue of the *New York Herald* which made a similar observation, noting that the animal was a typical specimen found grazing in the New York Zoological Park (more commonly known as the Bronx Zoo).[2]

Under the traditional story, however, Black Diamond was born in the Central Park Zoo, not the Bronx Zoo, in 1893 from Barnum & Bailey stock and lived until 1915. Or, in a slightly different version, he was a Barnum & Bailey circus buffalo, *retired* to the Central Park Zoo.

The December 1915 issue of *The Numismatist* also placed Black Diamond at Central Park. Reporting on the bison's death, the journal said:

Black Diamond, the aged buffalo, whose likeness is printed on our $10 legal tender notes and is stamped on the last issue of five-cent pieces, was put to death in New York on November 17. He was

The real name of the bison for the back of the Indian Head nickel remains in question.

★★★

about 20 years old and the largest bison in captivity. He had been an inmate of the Central Park corral for many years. Black Diamond's hide, which measured 13 by 13 feet, will be made into an automobile robe. The bison weighed 1,550 pounds, from which 750 pounds dressed meat was obtained. The teeth were in a remarkable state of preservation. The head, which will be mounted, sold for a considerable amount of money. The bison was killed because of old age. He was sold in the surplus live-stock auction last summer and was left at the park subject to the call of his purchaser.[3]

Missing flag

Where's the missing flag? When the Jefferson nickel was released, in 1938, a rumor spread quickly that the depiction of the White House on the coin's reverse was missing the U.S. flag. The coins would, no doubt, be recalled. The rush to obtain Jefferson nickels was on.

Problem was, the building is Monticello, Thomas Jefferson's home, not the White House.

The rumor apparently started, and was circulated by a prominent radio commentator, after the winning designs were released to the press.

This wasn't the only rumor linked to the Jefferson nickel's release; another claimed the coins were too wide to fit into subway slots and were being recalled.

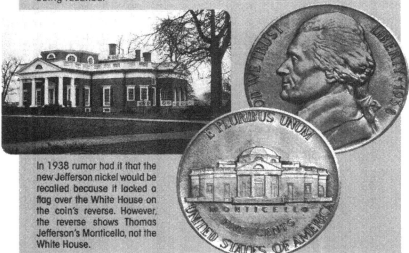

In 1938 rumor had it that the new Jefferson nickel would be recalled because it lacked a flag over the White House on the coin's reverse. However, the reverse shows Thomas Jefferson's Monticello, not the White House.

★★★

The price, by some accounts, was $700, with the carcass sold to A. Silz Poultry and Game. Silz had the head mounted and sold the meat as Black Diamond Steaks at good prices.

The head later came into the possession of Benjamin H. Mayer, an employee of Hoffman & Mayer Inc., the firm that took over from Silz. It remained on display at the firm until Hoffman & Mayer closed its doors in 1978. In 1985, the head was shown at the American Numismatic Association convention in Baltimore.

It may just be a case of a mixed-up identification by the artist and the *Herald* between the Bronx Zoo, a full-scale zoo, and the Central Park Menagerie (or corral), a small, penned-in display of animals, but even into the 1970s, when William Bridges (then curator of publications at the New York Zoological Society) wrote *Gathering of Animals: An Unconventional History of the New York Zoological Society,* the Bronx Zoo was still receiving queries as to Black Diamond, but could find no record of the zoo ever owning an animal by that name.

A sad failure

The confusion, Bridges said, could be traced as far back as William T. Hornaday, first director of the New York Zoological Park. Hornaday was responsible for bringing a herd of bison to the park to graze on a special 20-acre range.[4]

TAR AND FEATHERS

Adolph Weinman's eagle on his Walking Liberty half dollar was quickly attacked. Ornithologist Frank Chapman, charged that "the artist has made this bird a terrestrial fowl, striding or marching on the ground like a turkey-cock, and with as much dignity as one." Another critic lampooned the eagle's attire, saying, "the eagle looks as though it were wearing overalls and marching through hot tar."[1]

The eagle on the reverse of Adolph Weinman's much acclaimed Walking Liberty half dollar (1916-1947) was criticized.

★★★

In November 1915 one correspondent wrote to Hornaday:

> I see in the paper a notice of the death of the big
> bison 'Black Diamond,' or 'Toby' as he was familiarly
> known. It has been stated that Black Diamond was
> the model for the buffalo on the ten dollar bill, also
> the five-cent nickle [sic.] If that is so it does not do
> him justice and was enough to make him ill. Was
> Black Diamond in the Central Park collection of
> animals or was he in the Zoological Park? The paper
> stated he was confined in Central Park.[5]

Bridges could find no record of Hornaday's response. However,
to a similar inquiry, wanting to know how the animal came by its
name, Hornaday replied that the buffalo named Black Diamond was
a Central Park animal, which the Bronx Zoo had nothing to do with.
Hornaday added that it was possible the name had been bestowed
on an animal by Billy Snyder, Central Park's head keeper.[6]

Yet, he wondered, "if 'Black Diamond' was as fine an animal
as we are asked to believe, then I cannot understand why he
should be sold to a butcher at a cut price."

Hornaday was certain, however, that Black Diamond was not
the animal that served as the model for the $10 bill. Hornaday
said he visited the Smithsonian Institution when the glass front
of an exhibit of bison (which he mounted in the 1880s while
chief taxidermist at the Smithsonian) was removed so that
photographs could be taken in preparation of the new $10 bill.[7]

MISSING A LEG

There are many error/variety coins that bring premiums from collectors.
One of those long sought after by nickel collectors is the
1937-D "three-legged" Buffalo nickel. In this instance,
the bison on the coin's reverse appears to have only
three legs, as the bottom of the bison's right leg was
inadvertently ground off the die that struck the coins.
Genuine examples sell for several hundreds of dollars
even in low grades. There are other dates that sport
partial legs, and bring premiums, such as the 1936-D 3
½-legged coin, but none is more famous than the 1937-D
three-legged coin.

A popular variety is the 1937-D three-legged
Indian Head nickel.

★★★

WAR EAGLES

Of war and peace might be one way of describing the symbolism on U.S. coins. When U.S. Mint engraver Robert Scot adapted the Great Seal of the United States for use on the reverse of the nation's coinage, he changed the depiction to show the eagle with arrows (war) in its right, or honorable, claw and an olive branch (peace) in its left, or sinister, claw. This was apparently incorrect. If you were looking to keep the peace it would have been the other way around.

The war eagle depiction appears on Draped Bust half dimes (1800-1805), dimes (1798-1807), quarters (1804-1807), half dollars (1801-1807), silver dollars (1798-1804), Capped Bust right quarter eagles (1796-1807), Capped Bust right half eagles (1796-1807), and Capped Bust right eagles (1797-1804).

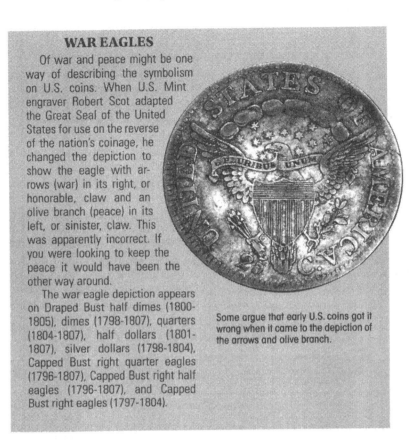

Some argue that early U.S. coins got it wrong when it came to the depiction of the arrows and olive branch.

Bridges also quoted a Jan. 7, 1918, letter from Martin S. Garretson, secretary of the Bison Society, to Hornaday in which the secretary was looking for a good picture of Black Diamond, the animal formerly in the Central Park Menagerie and believed to have been used on the Indian Head nickel.

Hornaday replied that the zoo had no information on the animal, but "judging from the character of the buffalo on the nickel, I should say from its dejected appearance" that the animal was likely an inmate of a small menagerie, having lived all of its life in a small enclosure.

"Its head droops as if it had lost all hope in the world, and even the sculptor was not able to raise it," Hornaday wrote. "I regard the bison on the nickel as a sad failure, considered as a

★★★

work of art."[8] Garretson, however, attributed the drooping head and tail to the sculptor's need to compress the animal in the coin design. Similarly, Edgar Adams, editor of *The Numismatist,* who placed Black Diamond as a specimen of the New York Zoological Garden, said:

> We have no doubt that the original enlarged model of this design was of a handsome character, but that it would not allow for the great reduction to the size of a five-cent piece is quite apparent.[9]

Bridges said additional confusion as to the possible location of a bison named Black Diamond is found in the aforementioned *New York Tribune* article, where the reporter observed that the animal was "grazing." Grazing, he said, would have been possible on the New York Zoological Park's 20 acres, but not at the Central Park Menagerie, which displayed its animals penned in, with no access to grass.

Bridges' theory was that Fraser may have inspected Black Diamond at the Central Park Menagerie, and, after finding him unsuitable, found a better animal at the Bronx Zoo — the dramatic name Black Diamond sticking in his mind when he talked of the model for the coin.[10]

A Bronx tale

Alas, the story should have but didn't end there. Slightly more than a decade after the announcement of Black Diamond's death, collectors were told that a different animal, ironically named Bronx, served as the model.

The August 1926 issue of *The Numismatist* strangely reported:

> Bronx, the buffalo whose portrait adorns the buffalo nickel, is no longer king of the Bronx Zoological Park herd, says a press dispatch. His thirty-five year reign ended recently when Cheyenne, a younger bull, challenged his leadership and, after a terrific battle, gored his right side and knocked off one of his horns. After the keepers separated the animals the deposed monarch was exiled to a separate pen and Cheyenne was left to lead the herd.[11]

* ✸ *

Chapter 3

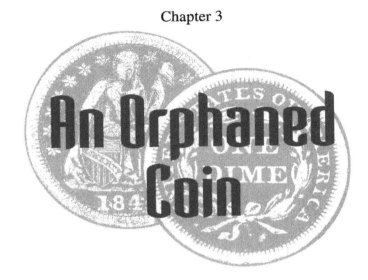

An Orphaned Coin

R eplete with its own colorful moniker, the 1844 dime may not be the scarcest Seated Liberty dime but it's certainly one of the most fabled, carrying with it an enchanting story of Mexican senoritas, lovesick soldiers and shiny bangles made of dimes.

Despite being scarce only in higher grades, the 1844 dime, with a mintage of 72,500, continues to attract attention, bringing good premiums in all grades. This is probably because of the promotional efforts of Frank C. Ross, a writer from the Kansas City area, who some believe provided the coin with the nickname "Orphan Annie," by which it is known today.[1]

Whether or not Ross was responsible for tagging the coin "Orphan Annie," it is certain he presented one of the most vivid accounts of a once popular rumor of how this dime came to be scarce. In a 1946 *Numismatic Scrapbook Magazine* article, Ross said that numismatists had been searching for years for the reason why 1844 dimes are rare. One of the most popular stories to emerge, he said, was that the coins went with the U.S. Army to Mexico, where the dimes were used to win sexual favors from Mexican senoritas.[2] The story went something like this...

★★★

Though not a great rarity, the 1844 "Orphan Annie" dime has a great story behind it.

In 1844, with a surplus of dimes on hand, the new sacked and counted 1844 dimes were placed in the corner of a Philadelphia Mint vault for future use. As dimes were needed, the coins were taken from rows at the front of the vault, thereby leaving the 1844 dimes undisturbed.

This probably would have remained the case if troops hadn't been mustered for an invasion of Mexico. The expedition's paymaster made requisition for a large supply of small change to be used by the soldiers. Thus, the 1844 dimes, conveniently bagged and counted, went with the soldiers to Mexico.

Once in Mexico's capital, the soldiers became homesick and longed for female companionship. It was then that one of their number came upon a plan to attract the local senoritas. Noticing that they liked to wear fancy bangles, he fashioned some bracelets using the 1844 dimes.

It worked. A booming enterprise followed as others in his company stumbled over each other, lining up to buy the bracelets. Not an 1844 dime

LIGHT UP

A note from an "S.T., Chicago" in the May 1945 issue of *The Numismatist* reported the discovery of an unusual 1944 Lincoln cent.

S.T. said of the coin, "With a strong magnifier I can see the faint outline of a cigarette in Lincoln's mouth." S.T. was obviously having more basic problems, as he also wrote, "If you want to please a lot of us collectors, you should print the 'Reports of Club Meetings' in a much larger type. They give me a lot of trouble."[1]

The editor suggested he get new glasses.

✱✱✱

WE ALL SCREAM

In 1894, there was an extremely low mintage of dimes at the San Fran-scisco Mint. Just 24 1894-S dimes were produced and today less than 10 are known to exist. One of the more inventive theories as to why so few of these were minted involved San Francisco Mint superintendent John Daggett and his daughter Hallie. Under this disputed telling, the coins were produced for Daggett's banking friends, with three specimens given to Hallie by her father with the admonishment to keep the coins until she was as old as he was. This being because he knew they would someday be valuable. However, on her way home from the Mint, Hallie spent one of the coins on a dish of ice cream.

Very few 1894-S dimes still exist. The original mintage was just 24 coins.

escaped the love-crazed surge. When the soldiers came home, the bracelets stayed behind with their new loves. But, like time, love is often fleeting. The soldiers were soon forgotten and the bracelets melted, the silver being reminted into Mexican coins.

This was just one of many legends developed by playful, overactive minds concerning the scarcity of 1844 dimes. Other equally ambitious tales were:

- The coins were improperly alloyed, so most of the mintage was melted at the Mint.

- The entire issue had been bought up by a speculator, few survived.

- A bank in New Orleans requisitioned Washington for $5,000 in dimes.

- Fifty-thousand were shipped by boat but lost in a storm.

- The coins were lost in the Great Chicago Fire.

LONELY HALF DIME

There was no record of an 1870-S half dime until 1978, when the only known specimen was found. Another example may exist in the cornerstone of the old San Francisco Mint, but this is unverified.

The only known 1870-S half dime was first put on display at the American Numismatic Association convention in Houston, Texas, having been purchased early in the year from a dealer who apparently didn't realize its rarity.

The only known example of the 1870-S half dime.

- The dimes gravitated to Pennsylvania and were swept away in the Great Johnstown Flood.

- Seventy thousand of the coins were sent overland to the forty-niners in California via the Santa Fee Trail. Along the way, the coins were seized by bandits who hid the loot. The bandits were later killed, taking their knowledge of the secret hiding place with them for eternity to their graves.[3]

★★★

The first Philadelphia Mint as it appeared in 1854.

Chapter 4

Made in America

How many official U.S. mints have there been in the United States since the first one opened in 1792? Well, there have been several proposed mints that never made it past the drawing board. However, the answer current stands at eight.

Philadelphia was established in 1792 and is still in operation (though, of course, not in the same building). Coins from this mint carried no mintmark to identify the location of minting until the war nickels of 1942-1945, which had a large "P" over the dome of Jefferson's Monticello on the coin's reverse. The "P" for Philadelphia next appeared on circulating coins in 1979 with the Susan B. Anthony mini-dollar and has been used regularly on U.S. denominations, except the cent, since 1980.

Gold and silver discoveries and westward expansion led to additional minting facilities in other cities. Among these "branch" mints were three established in 1838, largely as result of Southern gold discoveries. They were Charlotte, N.C. ("C" mintmark), Dahlonega, Ga. ("D" mintmark), and New Orleans ("O" mintmark).

Today the West Point Mint puts its "W" mintmark on coins.

★ ★ ★

Dahlonega and Charlotte only minted gold and closed in 1861, with the outbreak of the Civil War, and never reopened. New Orleans struck gold and silver coins. It survived the Civil War and operated until 1909.

In 1854, a few years after the California Gold Rush began, San Francisco got its first mint ("S" mintmark). It has minted gold, silver and copper coins. The San Francisco Mint lost its mint status in 1955 and regained it in 1988. It strikes much of the nation's proof coinage.

The Carson City Mint, a short distance from the Comstock Lode's bonanza mines, began operation in 1870 ("CC" mintmark). It struck gold and silver coins from 1870 to 1893 with gaps in between.

In 1906 the Denver Mint ("D" mintmark) swung open its doors and today remains a primary manufacturer of U.S. coins.

'D-LESS' CENT

Among U. S. cents, one of the dates, actually mintmarks — or perhaps more appropriately, a coin without a mintmark — that has caused the biggest row is the 1922 "plain" cent. Even today controversy remains as to how much if any of the "D" for "Denver" can show on the cent for it to qualify as a high-premium coin.

As no cents were struck in 1922 at the Philadelphia Mint, theories were quickly developed as to how the "D-less" cents could have come into being. These ranged from the work of an unscrupulous Mint employee to the mintmark having been left off the master die by mistake.

But, as the *Empire Investors Report* once noted, "No amount of wishful thinking will make a 1922 'plain' cent a 1922 'Philadelphia' cent."[1] The coin was the product of a clogged Denver Mint die.

The 1922 "no D" Lincoln cent.

One determined collector didn't care. The July 1937 issue of *The Numismatist* records a letter from Maurice D. Scharlack of Corpus Christi, Texas, who argued that, D or no D, all 1922 coins would bring a premium. He, therefore, socked away 25,000 in a wooden chest for a rainy day.[2]

Today, a similar minor minting variety would add only slight value to the coin. For the 1922 "plain" cent, however, its place in the lore of Lincoln cents and the hobby is secure.

★★★

In 1988 the bullion depository at West Point, in New York, which had been striking coins since the 1970s, was upgraded to mint status. Some of its issues, especially the proof mintings, carry its "W" mintmark.

The New Orleans Mint opened in 1838 and coined gold and silver coins into the first part of the 20th century.

The Charlotte Mint, which coined only gold.

A view of the "Granite Lady," the old San Francisco Mint.

★ ★ ★

FREE F.O.R.D.

A bizarre rumor circulating prior to World War I claimed that a person finding four U.S. dimes with the mintmarks F, O, R, and D would win a car from the Ford Motor Co. The story made its rounds through the general press, with one New York newspaper, the *Utica Herald Dispatch*, forced to explain:

> Because of the offer of a prize some firm is said to have made to any person who shall combine four different mint mark letters on 10-cent silver pieces, so as to spell a certain word of four letters, many Uticans are searching for the four coins that are said to bear these letters. Their search is hopeless. Two of the letters are 'F' and 'R.' There is no coin ever struck that bears either of these letters as a mint mark.[3]

The "O" and "D" were findable in "FORD" by looking at mintmarks on dimes, but not the "F" and "R."

The article went on to name the various mints and their mintmarks — Philadelphia (no mintmark), Charlotte (C), Carson City (CC), Dahlonega (D), San Francisco (S), New Orleans (O) and Denver (D) — to prove it couldn't be done.

It added, however, "the combination would-be prize winners are searching for can easily be formed from the legend 'United States of America' on the dimes" and other coins of the United States.[4]

★★★

Chapter 5

Make it in Quints

Shown is the 500 unit, or quint.

*F*ortunately for Americans, Thomas Jefferson prevailed in his argument for a decimal system of coinage, otherwise things would have been much worse and more complicated.

Prior to the foundation of the federal government, coinage in the Colonies was a hodgepodge.

The Articles of Confederation, in 1781, gave individual states the right to produce copper coins. Many states found this appealing, and merchants in the mid-1780s traded copper coins of Vermont, Connecticut, Massachusetts, New Jersey and New York. Not all were legal issues; various

Robert Morris.

★ ★ ★

entrepreneurs used this as an invitation to strike imitation state coppers and British halfpence. Mutilated and worn foreign coins also circulated in abundance, with a large amount of the silver arriving from Spain.

FAT MISTRESS

When Mint engraver John Reich's Capped Bust design for the nation's coinage began appearing on half dollars and $5 gold coins in 1807, baseless rumors spread that the artist had portrayed his "fat mistress" on the coins. Reich's robust Liberty later appeared on U.S. dimes and quarters as well.

The accounting system used by the states was derived from the British system of pounds, shillings and pence. Each state was allowed to set its own rates at which foreign gold and silver coins would trade in relation to the British pound.

In 1782 Robert Morris, newly named superintendent of finance, was appointed to head a committee to determine the values and weights of the gold and silver coins in circulation. Asked simply to draw up a table of values and weights, Morris took the opportunity to propose the establishment of a federal mint. In his Jan. 15, 1782, report (largely written by his assistant Gouverneur Morris), Morris noted that the exchange rates between the states were complicated.

He observed that a farmer in New Hampshire would be hard-pressed if asked to determine the value of a bushel of wheat in South Carolina. Morris recorded that an amount of wheat worth

WEIGHTY PROPOSAL

Tradition holds that John Hull of Boston became so wealthy from his issuance of Colonial Pine Tree shillings that when it came time for his daughter, Hannah, to marry Samuel Sewall, her marriage dowry was made up of her weight in freshly minted silver Pine Tree shillings, or about 500 British pounds, a considerable sum in those days.

Her husband later became a judge, presiding over Salem witchcraft trials, where he condemned 19 people to their deaths.

A Pine Tree shilling.

★★★

four shillings in his home state of New Hampshire would be worth 21 shillings and eightpence under the accounting system use in South Carolina.

Morris claimed these difficulties plagued not only farmers, but also were "perplexing to most Men and troublesome to all." Morris further pressed for the adoption of an American coin to solve the problems of the need for small change and debased foreign coins in circulation.

RUM SOAKED

One of the more interesting pieces within the U.S. Colonial series is an issue of copper tokens dated 1737 and 1739, known to collectors as Higley coppers. The first of these pure copper issues bore the legend "Value of Three Pence," but protests from the community eventually caused issuer John Higley to retain the Roman numeral III, but change the inscription to read "Value Me as You Please."

Tradition has it that Higley, an ingenious blacksmith with a taste for rum, made up the coins to support his drinking habit. Rum, you see, was threepence a glass in those days.

Higley's copper threepence.

SILVER CENTER

So, if you're in charge of a new mint and copper is in short supply, what do you do? In 1792 one solution contemplated to solve the problem was to put a silver plug at the center of each cent minted. The new coin could then be smaller in size, use less copper, and still have the proper intrinsic value. Copper would make up three-quarters of this and silver one-quarter.

Specimens of Henry Voight's silver-center cent exist but are extremely rare. Also known are unstruck planchets for the coins.

One idea to save on copper was to place a silver plug at the center of the cent.

★★★

WITCH PIECES

During the heyday of the witch trials in Salem, Mass., superstition held that if you carried a bent silver coin in your pocket it would ward off witches. This, some say, may account for bent examples of early Massachusetts Colonial coinage.

If it is true, it's likely Judge Sewall, who condemned several people to death for practicing witchcraft, found ready use for his wife's rumored dowry of silver Pine Tree shillings.

In essence, what he was advocating was a monometallic system based on silver. He said gold and silver had fluctuated throughout history, and because these fluctuations resulted in the more valuable metal leaving the country, any nation that adopted a bimetallic coinage was doomed to have gold or silver coins disappear from circulation.

Gouverneur Morris calculated the rate at which the Spanish dollar traded to the British pound in the various states. Leaving out South Carolina, because it threw off his calculations, Gouverneur Morris arrived at a common denominator of 1,440. Robert Morris, therefore, recommended a unit of value of 1/1,440, equivalent to a quarter grain of silver. He suggested the striking of a silver 100-unit coin or cent; a silver 500-unit coin, or quint; a silver 1,000-unit coin, or mark; and two copper coins, one of eight units and the other of five units.

A COIN FOR THE POOR

First Treasury Secretary Alexander Hamilton is generally credited with the introduction of the half cent. This unusual denomination was the nation's lowest in circulation. Hamilton argued, in his 1791 "Report on the Establishment of a Mint," that it would aid the poor by allowing merchants to lower prices. Half cents were issued in spurts from 1793-1857 with gaps in the years of issue.

Alexander Hamilton is generally credited with the idea for the nation's lowest circulating denomination, the half cent.

★★★

Chapter 6

A Questionable Past

Just five examples of the 1913
Liberty Head nickel are known.

*I*t's probably every collector's dream to own a truly rare coin — a coin that only a few, if any, can possess, one rich in history and appeal. It is that spirit, that drive to obtain the obtainable, that has led to the fascinating story of the famed 1913 Liberty Head nickel, a coin that has passed through the hands of the lowly to the collection of a king to become a million-dollar-plus coin.

* ★ *

Worthy plot

The story of the origin and rise in popularity of the 1913 Liberty Head nickel is laced with so much mystery, loosely-based tales of chicanery, and endearing, colorful characters that a Hollywood scriptwriter would be hard-pressed to find a more interesting plot. Among the cast of characters are Col. Edward Howland Robinson Green, son of miserly Hetty Green, the "Witch of Wall Street"; King Farouk, overweight, overbearing playboy ruler of Egypt; Texas coin dealer B. Max Mehl, famous within coin circles for his self-benefiting 1913 Liberty Head nickel reward; and J.V. McDermott, a Milwaukee coin dealer who loved a good drink about as much as he loved his famous "MacNickel."

There are other characters, as well, all gathered within the folds of a story that began in 1912 and continues to this day. For those schooled in the ways of numismatics, it's an old story. It's the tale of how five examples of a design that was officially retired after 1912 — the Liberty Head by Charles Barber — came to be clandestinely struck at the U.S. Mint in Philadelphia. The culprit, according to legend, was Samuel W. Brown who, it is said, was involved in striking and bringing the illegitimate coins to the 1920 American Numismatic Association convention in Chicago, apparently to stir interest in a future sale.

Texas dealer B. Max Mehl is credited with helping to popularize the 1913 Liberty Head nickel.

His marketing campaign successful, Brown disappeared from the numismatic scene, presumably having found a purchaser. The coins next surfaced in 1924 in the possession of Philadelphia dealer August Wagner, later going (apparently as a group) to Col. Green. After Green's death, the coins were dispersed to a number of buyers.

⋆✶⋆

Unknown origins

Certainties are anything but the case in the story behind the creation of the 1913 Liberty Head nickel. What can be said reliably is very limited.

The exact date of the striking of these illegitimate coins has never been determined. Some believe it may have been as late as 1918. The majority contend the surreptitious minting must have happened in late 1912, before the release of James Earle Fraser's Indian Head nickel.

Noted researcher R.W. Julian, who had access to Mint documents subsequently destroyed, has effectively argued the latter theory — claiming that if the coins were struck prior to the release of the Indian Head nickel, the striking would need to have taken place sometime following the December 1912 order to change to James Earle Fraser's Indian Head nickel design and before a general defacement of outdated dies at year's end. Julian was able to substantiate the existence of 1913-dated Liberty Head nickel dies through records of a shipment to the San Francisco Mint. The shipment was made prior to the decision to change to the Indian Head nickel design.[1]

J.V. McDermott was said to have conducted much of his business at the bar. Here he is behind a bourse table.

Others, however, point to the lapse of time between 1913, the year the Indian Head nickel was released, and Brown's 1920 visit to the ANA convention as being suspect. They contend the coins could have been produced much later than 1913, perhaps by a Mint guard rumored to have been let go under mysterious circumstances in 1918.

* ★ *

Aubrey Bebee, a Nebraska dealer, who purchased McDermott's nickel in 1967 and later donated it to the American Numismatic Association.

A cash offer

Hobbyists apparently first learned of the possible existence of a 1913-dated Liberty Head nickel through the December 1919 issue of *The Numismatist,* where Brown offered to pay $500 in cash for an example, "in Proof condition, if possible." He ran a similar advertisement in the January 1920 issue, upping his offer to $600 per coin.

On Monday, Aug. 23, 1920, he attended the opening day of the ANA's four-day convention in Chicago, where he displayed at least one example of the 1913 Liberty Head nickel and told of the existence of five such coins. The October 1920 issue of *The Numismatist* notes:

> Samuel W. Brown of North Tonawanda, N.Y., was present for a short time on Monday. He had with him a specimen of the latest great rarity in U.S. coinage — the nickel of 1913 of the Liberty Head type. It was among the exhibits the remainder of the Convention, with a label announcing that it was valued at $600, which amount Mr. Brown announced he is ready to pay for all proof specimens offered to him.[2]

Brown explained that, at the close of 1912, the Mint had not yet received orders to use the Indian Head nickel dies and had prepared a "master die" of the Liberty Head design, dated 1913. From this master die, Brown said, a few specimens, "believed to be five," were struck in proof, none of which were thought to have been placed into circulation.

Upon his departure from the convention, Brown left the coin in the care of Chicago Coin Club president Alden Scott Boyer. It was placed on display until Aug. 26, 1920, the date the convention closed.

★★★

A few months later, Brown requested that Boyer return the nickel, as a sale was pending. Brown wrote:

> Dear Mr. Boyer — I would appreciate it very much if you would return the 1913 Liberty head nickel you have with your coins in the Masonic Temple vault in your city. I have a deal pending for the sale of this coin, and it is necessary that I have it within the next ten days. If you will, kindly send it to me express, charges collect, and estimate the value at $750. Thanking you for your courtesy in this matter.[3]

Thus, according to the most widely accepted theory, Brown had created an artificial rarity, developed a market for the coin, and eventually sold one or all five specimens.

A clever ruse

Who was Samuel Brown? How did he gain access to the Mint? Where did he obtain an appreciation for coins as being rare and collectible?

The answers to these questions — important in determining Brown's role in the story — were supplied by Don Taxay, who discovered that Brown had been employed by the Philadelphia Mint as an assistant curator of its coin cabinet from 1904 to 1907 and as a clerk/storekeeper until he left the Mint's employ in 1913. In 1906, Brown joined the ANA.

Supposition holds that Brown, with his knowledge of coin collecting (gained through his ANA membership and term as assistant curator at the Mint), was most culpable in the creation of the 1913 Liberty Head nickel. His advertisements in *The Numismatist*, it is said, were only a clever ruse, and when he arrived at the ANA convention he already had all five coins with him. (Some writers go so far as to add the colorful notation that he brought the coins to the

> **NICKEL EPIDEMIC**
>
> Since the hobby first learned of the existence of five 1913 Liberty Head nickels, there have been rumors of a missing sixth example. The hobby got more than it bargained for, however, when rewards from Texas dealer B. Max Mehl and the eccentric Col. E.H.R. Green began appearing in the 1930s. No additional genuine examples were found. However, fakes began popping up all over the place.

★ ★ ★

REAL RACKETEERS

Some collectors have come to believe that "original" plated Racketeer nickels — those made up in the 1800s to pass as $5 gold coins — can be distinguished from later alterations by the presence or lack of a reeded edge. This, of course, ignores the possibility that modern plated versions could also be reeded.

In 1960 a collector warned readers of *Numismatic Scrapbook Magazine* that Racketeer nickels of his day were strictly phoney. Modern con men don't take the trouble to reed the edge, he said. Rather, they buy 1883 "no cents" nickels at 35 cents each, plate the coins with five cents worth of gold, and sell the "new" Racketeer nickels to suckers at $2 to $5 each.

"I believe that he makes the old time crooks look like real pikers," he said of the modern fakers.[1]

The 1883 "no cents" Liberty Head nickel.

convention in a special holder, but there is no proof of this. Such a holder exists, but its origin is unclear.)

Unfortunately, no written record apparently exists proving Brown had all five coins *at* the convention, that he knew of their location, or that he already possessed all five. That Brown knew of the existence of five specimens is obvious from the reference in the October 1920 issue of *The Numismatist*. However, despite what countless writers have said, only one specimen has truly been accounted for as being at the convention.

The difference is, at first glance, a minor one. Brown may, after all, have had possession of the other four coins and simply failed to bring the complete set to the convention. Or, less likely, the editor of *The Numismatist* failed to correctly identify the number of 1913 Liberty Head nickels on display.

But the possibility exists that Brown's ads in *The Numismatist* were not a complete hoax — that knowing of the existence of other 1913 Liberty Head nickels, either because he was involved in or simply aware of the striking, Brown was genuinely hoping to obtain the remaining specimens before anyone else did.

★★★

Guilt by association

The point to remember, when assessing the damning charges consistently leveled against Brown, is that the case against him is based primarily on circumstantial evidence. Playing the same game, one can easily paint an entirely different picture of Brown and his activities in relation to these unauthorized rarities.

In his article, "Coin of Chance, Coin of Change, Coin of Conspiracy," in the May 1975 issue of *Coins* magazine, Julian made the reasonable observation that Brown couldn't have been alone in the production of these illegitimate coins. He wrote:

> The person responsible for actually striking the 1913 liberty head nickels almost certainly was in the engraver's department or an employee of the medal room itself, with the latter being the best bet. There

HOLLYWOOD BOUND

There have been a number of instances where coins and paper money have appeared in movies and in dramas and comedies on television. Most of the time it's in the form of prop money and generally not employing a true rarity. This wasn't the case, though, in the early 1970s when a real example of the five-known 1913 Liberty Head nickels was used in an episode of the CBS show "Hawaii Five-0," starring Jack Lord with Victor Buono as a special guest star.

Worth at the time around $175,000, the coin, then owned by World-Wide Coin Investments, was featured in an episode titled "$100,000 nickel." CBS taped part of the episode in Hawaii. However, the sequence with the 1913 nickel was filmed in Hollywood, with the coin being delivered to the set via a Brink's truck. It was to be used in close-ups and was briefly handled (by the edges) by Buono. In the episode, the coin is stolen and Five-0 is given the job of recovering it.

Victor Buono holds a real 1913 Liberty Head nickel in a promotional shot for an episode of "Hawaii Five-0."

★★★

were at least two men in on the plot, because the man who sold them some years later [Brown], although a former mint employee, did not work in the key area required for access to the proof dies.[4]

1942 ZINC CENT?

Does a pure zinc 1942 cent exist? According to a report in the March 6, 1973, issue of *Numismatic News*, citing an unidentified Mint source, such coins were struck in Philadelphia in 1942 as a test for a substitute for copper. "A couple of handfuls' of solid zinc cents were struck at Philadelphia in 1942, the mint source said, as part of the experiments to find a replacement for copper — then badly needed for the war effort," the *News* wrote. "Afterward, when the coins were counted, one was missing — and an immediate, thorough search failed to turn up it up." In 1943 the Mint did strike zinc-coated steel cents for one year.

The striking, Julian argues, must have occurred within a few days of Dec. 16, 1912, the date orders went out to the San Francisco Mint to return the 1913-dated dies sent to that mint in November 1912.

"The conspirators surely knew that the 1913 liberty head dies were liable for return to the engraver's department for destruction at any moment, and no time was to be lost if they were to have the only such coins," Julian wrote.[5]

If Julian's contention is correct — if Brown was involved in striking the coins, he must had an accomplice — it could just as easily be suggested that Brown may not have obtained *all* of the specimens upon leaving the Mint. Wouldn't his co-conspirator have wanted to keep one or more of the coins?

Model citizen

Using circumstantial evidence, it could also be argued that Brown's "model citizen" life after leaving the Mint proves he was totally above such chicanery and was an honored and respected citizen who has been wrongly indicted, tried, convicted and sentenced by the numismatic community without due process.

Reporting on Brown's death, the August 1944 issue of *The Numismatist* told that Brown, a native of Pennsylvania, served several terms as mayor of North Tonawanda, N.Y., spent 10 years on the board of education, and once served on the U.S. Assay Commission.[6]

★★★

An obituary notice in the June 19, 1944, issue of the North Tonawanda *Evening News* adds additional biographical information on Brown. Noting that Brown (age 64 at the time of his death) was a Republican, the *News* said Brown served as mayor of North Tonawanda from 1932-1933, having moved to that city in 1913 to go into association with Wayne Fahnestock in Frontier Chocolate Co. Later Brown was employed by Pierce-Brown Co., retiring in 1924.

Brown was a member of Sutherland Lodge No. 826, of the Free and Accepted Masons, of which he was past master. He also served as district deputy grandmaster of the Niagara Oleans district and was a member of the Buffalo consistory, the Ismailia Temple and the Shrine Club of Tonawanda.[7]

Do these sound like the credentials of a nefarious character? Of course not. Does it prove that Brown was innocent of the charges numismatists have made against him? No, it doesn't. The point is, Brown has been convicted by association, not on the basis of hard facts.

It's a charge that will likely stick, even though what really happened may never be known. Left to the fertile imaginations of those who look for nefarious motives in every human action, the story will continue to be a murky mirror of the truth, at best.

Fit for a king

By 1924 all five specimens of the 1913 Liberty Head nickel had come into August Wagner's possession. An ad by Wagner in the December 1923 issue of *The Numismatist* advised:

> FOR SALE. Five (5) Liberty Head 1913 Coins. Proof. The only Five-Cent Liberty Head Coins of this design and year in existence.

The coins then passed through various hands to the eccentric Col. E.H.R. Green, who readily lavished money on his collectibles. Born in London on Aug. 22, 1868, Green was the son of Edward Howland Robinson Green. He was raised, however, by his wealthy mother, Hetty Green, whose miserly ways came to the fore when her son injured his leg in a sledding accident at the age of 9. Legend has it, she refused to call a doctor, preferring to save money by treating his injury herself.

* * *

Two years later, when he re-injured the leg, she dressed the boy in rags and took him from free clinic to free clinic. When a doctor found out who she was and demanded payment, she refused. Some years later, the leg had to be amputated.

Hetty Green, who was once termed the "Witch of Wall Street."

As much as his mother liked to squirrel money away, her son enjoyed spending it. According to Arthur H. Lewis in *The Day They Shook the Plum Tree,* the 6-foot 4-inch, 300-pound Green spent nearly $3 million a year on yachts, coins, stamps, jewels and other dalliances.

In a mimic of a successful sales promotion by Texas coin dealer B. Max Mehl, Green once offered $10,000 for anyone discovering an additional 1913 Liberty Head nickel. It was a reward he knew full well would never have to be paid.[8]

Mehl had already made the rarity famous through a series of radio and press promotions, offering to pay $50 for anyone discovering a new 1913 Liberty Head nickel. The gimmick paid off in new clients for his rare coin business but not in new nickels.

Following Green's death, in 1936, the coins next came into the possession of either dealer Burdette Johnson or collector Eric P. Newman. The exact ownership details are a bit foggy. Although Johnson is generally credited as being the next in line to receive all five coins, Newman said, in an interview with this writer, that he once owned all of the coins. The June 1961 issue of *Numismatic Scrapbook Magazine* notes similarly that "before the late B.G. Johnson split up the set in the Green estate, Eric P. Newman had all specimens in his possession . . ."[9]

★★★

Newman kept at least one specimen, which later went to dealer Abe Kosoff and found its way to Ambassador R. Henry Norweb and his wife. It currently resides in the collection of the Smithsonian Institution.

At one point, two specimens were owned by Egypt's playboy ruler, King Farouk. According to Kosoff, who chronicled the sale of the king's collection in a series of articles for *Coin World*, Farouk (whose extravagances ran from sex to gambling to eclectic collections) obtained the Fred C. Boyd specimen of the rarity from Kosoff and had, at about the same time, placed a successful bid for a different example in Mehl's sale of the Fred Olsen collection.[10]

King Farouk of Egypt amassed a large collection of coins, which included a 1913 Liberty Head nickel.

According to Kosoff, Farouk commissioned Mehl to sell the additional specimen. When Farouk abdicated in 1952, the royal collection was put up for sale. The sale, held two years later, was the landmark numismatic event of its day, with many prominent dealers and numismatists making the trip to Egypt to bid on the collection's extensive U.S. holdings. The 1913 Liberty Head nickel went for just under $4,000.[11]

Another specimen was with dealer George O. Walton, in 1962, when the dealer lost his life in a car crash. The coin was recovered at the time, but misidentified as a fake. Its continued existence wasn't known until 2003, when it was brought by Walton's relatives to the ANA convention in Baltimore, compared with the other examples, and pronounced genuine by a group of professional numismatists.

MacNickel

The most colorful and endearing owner of a 1913 Liberty Head was J.V. McDermott, a hard-drinking, vest-pocket dealer from Milwaukee who was known for sliding "MacNickel" down the bar for the curious to see. McDermott purchased his specimen of the 1913 Liberty Head nickel from Jim Kelly in the early 1940s for $900 and quickly made himself and the nickel famous.

* ★ *

Even today, many numismatists have cherished stories to tell of their meetings with McDermott and of his rare nickel. Such is the case with collector Tom Fruit, who as a child became a friend and sometimes caretaker of the famous coin.

Fruit, 14 at the time, met McDermott in 1949 after Fruit's family moved to the south part of Milwaukee. A coin collector, Fruit became intrigued when he learned that a famous coin dealer lived not too far from his house. He went right over and knocked on the back door, where he was greeted by McDermott, clad in a sleeveless T-shirt.

"He was really nice," Fruit said. "I told him I was interested in collecting coins, so he reached into his pocket and pulled out a Pine Tree Shilling and his 1913 nickel."[12]

Fruit became a regular patron of McDermott's, going back to make purchases from the dealer whenever a spare $5 or $10 earned from an odd job allowed.

For a young collector, the association was a dream come true — a wealth of coins only a few feet from his family's home. The two became friends. When Fruit turned 16 and was able to drive, he often drove McDermott to coin club meetings and coin shows.

"He would drive there and I'd drive back, because he did most of his business at the bar," Fruit said of McDermott. "He never had a table that I remember. His table was the bar."

McDermott made no secret of his passion for drinking, and often made reference to it at the beginning of his advertisements in *Numismatic Scrapbook Magazine.* In the February 1950 issue he said: "Had a bad cold last month. Doc says, 'Go to bed for a couple of days.' But I didn't[,] as long as I can lift my arm and bend an elbow. I['ll] never give up."

From the February 1954 issue came: "That Dan Brown guy out in Denver told me of a rumor that's goin' around to whit that they're goin' to make us eat our corn instead of drink it — it's very disturbing."

And from the September 1960 issue: "Had to miss the Boston show — my neck looked like a hunk of raw meat (reaction from those x-ray treatments I guess). Looks like I'll have some surgery. Oh! Me! Some of my pals want to get a pool going and one tavern-keeper has offered to mount my head behind his

★

bar. (He says — as a warning to others.) Another one says he thinks it would be better if they shrink it. Anyway, I may fool them if lucky."

Fruit remembers taking the famous coin to school to have pictures taken for McDermott.

"I used to carry that nickel around for days at a time," he said. "I'd carry it around in my pocket. He wasn't afraid to give it to anybody.

"A lot of times, at a coin show, he didn't know where it was. It would be circulated up and down the bar and somebody would have it. Anytime I wanted the nickel, he would just give it to me. He didn't ask any questions."

McDermott also freely loaned the coin to clubs to promote their coin shows. Some believe, however, that with the number of venues at which the coin appeared, McDermott must have had a duplicate made. Fruit discounts such stories.

> **WHO'S JOSHING WHOM?**
>
> A favorite story among numismatists is that the popular phrase of disbelief "you're joshing" originated with Josh Tatum and his passing of plated nickels as $5 gold coins. Sorry, as writer Eric von Klinger pointed out, its origin dates to much earlier.
>
> The *American Thesaurus of Slang*, for example, notes of "josh": "To banter, kid (U.S.-1845). Origin obscure. The earliness of the usage rules out the supposition that it derives from 'Josh Billings,' who had not yet gained a reputation as a humorist."[2] So it does with Josh Tatum.

"There was a lot of talk that Mac had the real nickel and then a replica of it, and that is not true," he said. "There has never been any substantiation to that.

"In fact, I know it is not true, because I could recognize that nickel today. It had a little dent or flake missing right underneath the [Liberty's] jaw. So I could recognize that nickel anytime, and it was always the same nickel.

"I think the reason for that is, people thought that he would never let a coin that expensive out of his sight. But that didn't bother him because, he said, 'What good is it to anybody. Everybody knows where the five nickels are and everybody knows that there are only five. Any one that would turn up, if it was stolen, nobody could sell it, because they would know whose it was.' So that is why he really wasn't concerned about anybody swiping it, and nobody ever did."

* ★ *

Even after Fruit moved away from Milwaukee, he found that McDermott was willing to loan him the coin (at that point valued at nearly $12,500) for display at coin shows.

McDermott's attitude toward loaning his valuable coin out for others to enjoy can be seen in an article he wrote for *Coins* magazine shortly before his death.

"I don't believe this coin, or any rarity, should be perpetually consigned to the concealing darkness of a bank vault," McDermott said. "Legally one man may 'own' this 1913 Liberty head nickel, but in a very real sense it belongs to numismatics; for should the collecting fraternity lose interest in it the 1913 would fall by the wayside — all five would be required to buy a handi-pack of not-so-good five cent cigars."[13]

McDermott died on Sept. 29, 1966. The obituary notice in *The Numismatist* said, "He had myriad friends but few, if any, intimates," but he "will live long in the memory of many who saw him and 'it' from coast to coast."[14]

Following her husband's death, McDermott's wife, Elizabeth, consigned the coin to a sale held Aug. 8, 1967, during the ANA convention in Miami, where it sold for a then amazing price of $46,000 to Nebraska dealer Aubrey Bebee, who later donated it to the ANA Money Museum in Colorado Springs, Colo.

By 2007, the fame and value of the 1913 Liberty Head nickels had grown to the point where the finest-known specimen was sold for a reported $5 million — a big price for a small coin with an uncertain past but a million-dollar-plus future.

★★★

Chapter 7

Religious Motto

*T*he battle over the use of the motto "In God We Trust" on U.S. currency is a never-ending one. Just about each and every year a suit is filed in a federal court by those who object its use, and each and every year it is defeated.

In the early 1900s, however, debate raged not because of its placement on U.S. coins but its deletion, as protests were raised over the release of the "godless" gold $10 and $20 designed by Augustus Saint-Gaudens.

Rev. M.R. Watkinson suggested the use of a religious motto on U.S. coins. He called for "God, Liberty and Law" to appear on the nation's coins.

The oft-told story is that President Theodore Roosevelt objected to the use of the deity on a coin as being sacrilegious. It was, therefore, omitted from the 1907 and some 1908 eagles as well as the 1907 double eagles.

Although it is true that Roosevelt issued a lengthy statement defending the decision to leave the religious motto off the new gold coins, this was only part of the story — a story of an artist who believed simplicity of design essential and of a president who defended this position.

★ ★ ★

This 1863 two-cent pattern carries the motto "God and Our Country."

Motto's first use

The motto "In God We Trust" was first introduced on U.S. coins with the two-cent piece of 1864. Its placement there is credited to Rev. M.R. Watkinson, minister of the gospel, Ridleyville, Pa., who suggested honoring the deity, in some form, on the nation's currency.

Watkinson wrote in a Nov. 13, 1861, letter to Treasury Secretary Salmon P. Chase that:

> You are about to submit your annual report to Congress respecting the affairs of the national finances.
>
> One fact touching our currency has hitherto been seriously overlooked. I mean the recognition of the Almighty God in some form in our coins.[1]

Watkinson worried that, if the nation was shattered beyond reconstruction by the Civil War, antiquaries of following centuries looking at the nation's coins would conclude the United States was a heathen nation.

> What I propose is that instead of the goddess of liberty, we shall have next inside the 13 stars a ring inscribed with the words 'perpetual union;' within this ring the all-seeing eye, crowned with a halo; beneath this eye the American flag, bearing in its field stars to the number of States united; in the folds of the bars the words 'God, liberty, law.'[2]

★★★

The two-cent piece as issued in 1864 became the first U.S. coin to use "In God We Trust."

Chase agreed, in principle, writing to Mint Director James Pollock on Nov. 20, 1861, and calling for placement of "a motto expressing in the fewest and tersest words possible this national recognition."[3]

Several variations of the motto were proposed and tried by Mint engraver James B. Longacre, including "Our Trust is in God," "God Our Trust," "God Trust," and "God is our Trust."

It wasn't, however, until a Dec. 9, 1863, letter from Chase to Pollock in regard to the new two-cent coin that Chase suggested "In God We Trust" be used. Failing this, he proposed "God is Our Shield."

Following its first use on the two-cent piece, an act passed in 1865 allowed the Mint director to place the motto "In God We Trust" on U.S. coins at his discretion. In 1866 it was added to all silver and gold coins, with the exception of the dime, half dime and three-cent piece, which were omitted due to size. Use of the motto was continued by the Coinage Act of 1873 and eventually adopted for lower denomination U.S. coins.

SEEING STARS

Why are there 94 stars between the denticles (tooth-like projections) on the reverse of some 1794 Liberty Cap cents? Theories range from an engraver having too much time on his hands to their use as a counterfeiting deterrent. Either way, the 1794 star-reverse cent is a famous if curious rarity.

★ ★ ★

First examples of Augustus Saint-Gaudens' gold $10s and $20s caused a stir when they left off the motto "In God We Trust."

The price of omission

In 1905 President Theodore Roosevelt commissioned renowned sculptor Augustus Saint-Gaudens to take on the task of redesigning the nation's gold coinage.

Saint-Gaudens asked the legal requirements concerning the motto "In God We Trust" and other inscriptions in a Nov. 22, 1905, letter to Treasury Secretary L.M. Shaw, enclosing a copy to Roosevelt. Saint-Gaudens observed that law required an impression "emblematic of liberty, with the inscription of the word 'liberty' and the year of coinage" and asked if he could add the word "justice" or "law" to his design. He also queried whether authorization was in place requiring the placement of "In God We Trust" on the coinage.[4]

★★★

Shaw's reply is unknown, though it's likely no objection to the omission of the motto was forwarded to the artist, even though legal requirements existed.

Roosevelt, likewise, made no reference to Saint-Gaudens' concerns regarding the motto, saying only of Saint-Gaudens' design:

> This is first class. I have no doubt we can get permission to put on the word 'Justice,' and I firmly believe that you can evolve something that will not only be beautiful from the artistic standpoint, but that, between the very high relief of the Greek and the very low relief of the modern coins, will be adapted both to the mechanical necessities of our mint production and the needs of modern commerce, and yet will be worthy of a civilized people — which is not true of our present coins.[5]

Saint-Gaudens had written to Roosevelt years earlier (in relation to his design for Roosevelt's inaugural medal) that simplicity of inscription was preferable in artistic designs. He apparently felt similarly in his work on the new gold coins.[6]

His son, Homer Saint-Gaudens, related in a 1920 article for *Century Illustrated Monthly Magazine* that the problem of including the authorized inscriptions was a difficult one, requiring the use of a date on each coin, the word "Liberty," "E Pluribus Unum," the legend "In God We Trust," inclusion of 13 stars to represent the original Colonies, 46 stars for the states then in the Union and "United States of America." Homer Saint-Gaudens wrote:

President Theodore Roosevelt was against the use of "In God We Trust" on the new gold coins by Augustus Saint-Gaudens.

* ★ *

The suggestion of the word 'Justice' was given up. In the case of the twenty-dollar gold piece the thirteen stars and the 'E. Pluribus Unum,' and in the case of the ten-dollar gold piece the forty-six stars, were placed upon the previously milled edges of the coin. The 'In God we trust' was discarded as an inartistic intrusion not required by law. The President gave his sanction to placing the date of the coinage in Roman instead of Arabic figures. The word 'Liberty,' the denomination of the coin, and the 'United States of America' alone remained to be dealt with. The situation seemed clarified.

Salmon P. Chase, Treasury secretary from 1861-1864.

Unfortunately, however, the removal of the 'In God we trust' drew down the lightning of public disapproval. The burden of the complaint was that the dropping of the legend was irreligious, although in this connection it was amusing to discover that Salmon P. Chase, who was Lincoln's secretary of the treasury, sustained quite as stern a censure for placing these words upon the coins as was aroused by their removal. The President, with his usual delight in a fight, took the onus of this charge upon himself and stood the tempest remarkably well; but at a later date, the sculptor being dead, and Mr. Roosevelt no longer in a position to prevent it, the authorities in the mint reverted to their own sweet way, with the result that 'In God we trust' and the Arabic numerals reappeared on the Saint-Gaudens's coins, to the increased impairment of whatever of worth in the original design had been allowed to remain.[7]

★★★

Roosevelt reacts

Publicly Roosevelt defended the position, saying in a Nov. 13, 1907, letter:

> When the question of the new coinage came up we looked into the law and found there was no warrant for putting 'In God We Trust' on the coins. As the custom, although without legal warrant has grown up, however, I might have felt at liberty to keep the inscription had I approved of its being on the coinage. But as I did not approve of it, I did not direct that it should again be put on.
>
> Of course the matter of the law is absolutely in the hands of congress and any direction of congress in the matter will be immediately obeyed. At present as I have said, there is no warrant in law for the inscription.
>
> My own feeling in the matter is due to my very firm conviction that to put such a motto on coins or to use it in any kindred manner, not only does no good but does positive harm, and is in effect irreverence which comes dangerously close to sacrilege. A beautiful and solemn sentence such as the one in question should be treated and uttered with that fine reverence which necessarily implies a certain exaltation of spirit.
>
> Any use which tends to cheapen it, and above all, any use which tends to secure its being treated in a spirit of levity, is from every standpoint profoundly to be regretted. It is a motto which is indeed well to have inscribed in our great national monuments, in our temples of justice, in our legislative halls, and in buildings such as those at West Point and Annapolis — in short, wherever it will tend to arouse and inspire a lofty emotion in those who look thereon. But it seems to me

WORTH A MILLION

What was the first U.S. coin to bear the motto "In God We Trust"? This question was used in one of the upper-level rounds of the popular quiz show "Who Wants to be a Millionaire." The answer is the two-cent piece, issued from 1864-1873.

* ★ *

eminently unwise to cheapen it by use on postage stamps, or in advertisements.

As regards its use on coinage, we have actual experience by which to go. In all my life I have never heard any human being speak reverently of this motto on the coins, or show any sign of its having appealed to any high emotion in him, but I have literally hundreds of times heard it used as an occasion of, and incitement to the sneering ridicule which it is above all things undesirable that so beautiful and exalted a phrase should excite.

For example, throughout the long contest extending over several decades on the free coinage question, the existence of this motto on the coins was a constant source of jest and ridicule; and this was unavoidable. Everyone must remember the innumerable cartoons and articles based on phrases like 'In God We Trust for the Eight Cents,' 'In God We Trust for the Short Weight,' 'In God We Trust for the Thirty-seven Cents We do not Pay,' etc., etc. Surely I am well within bounds when I say that a use of the phrase which invites constant levity of this type is most undesirable. If congress alters the law and directs me to replace on the coins the sentence in question, the direction will be immediately put into effect, but I very earnestly trust that the religious sentiment of the country, the spirit of reverence in the country will prevent any such action being taken.[8]

Roosevelt was wrong. On May 18, 1908, Congress passed an act requiring the motto's restoration. Today it continues to appear on U.S. coins and has found a place on the nation's paper money as well.

★★★

Chapter 8

A Perfect Model

*I*f you've been a collector for some time, you've probably heard that an Irish lass, Mary Cunningham, served as the model for Augustus Saint-Gaudens' graceful, striding figure of Liberty on the gold double eagle, released in 1907. Failing that, you've been told Alice Butler modeled for the coin, or that Saint-Gaudens' mistress, Davida Clark, should be so honored.

You've probably never heard of Hettie Anderson, or maybe you have, only in a rather vague and often overlooked reference. She's the "woman supposed to have negro blood in her veins" once referred to by the artist's son, Homer Saint-Gaudens, as a possible model.

It probably wouldn't have sat too well with the blue bloods of Homer Saint-Gaudens' day if they found out that a black woman served as a model for the nation's $20 gold coin. However, it now appears the Saint-Gaudens double eagle may indeed have been modeled after Hettie Anderson, an African-American woman from New York.

Augustus Saint-Gaudens died prior to the release of his gold $20s.

Photograph by D.C. Ward.

★ ★ ★

This discovery was made in 1991 by William E. Hagans, a relative of Anderson's, and was first published in Krause Publications' weekly newspaper for coin collectors, *Numismatic News*.

Saint-Gaudens, the artist

To learn the story of Anderson and her modeling for Saint-Gaudens is to learn of an artist who fervently believed, as did President Theodore Roosevelt, that the nation's coinage should be raised to a loftier artistic standard — similar to the impressive high-relief, hand-struck coins of ancient Greece.

By his own account, published as *The Reminiscences of Augustus Saint-Gaudens,* Saint-Gaudens was born on March 1, 1848, in Dublin, Ireland, to Bernard and Mary (McGuiness) Saint-Gaudens.

His family emigrated to America shortly after his birth. Arriving in late 1848, they settled in New York, where his father was engaged in manufacturing shoes.

In 1861, Saint-Gaudens, then 13, began the formal pursuit of a career in art, finding work producing cameos as an apprentice for New York stone cameo-cutter Louis Avet during the day (a period described by Saint-Gaudens as years "of miserable slavery") and taking art classes at the Cooper Institute at night.

Leaving Avet, in 1864, Saint-Gaudens took employment with another stonecutter, Jules Le Brethen, a shell cameo-cutter for whom he worked the following three years while engaging in additional art studies at the National Academy of Design.

GERM RIDDEN

One of the most interesting U.S. coin designs is the sunken design by Bela Lyon Pratt for the gold $2.50 and $5 coins, issued beginning in 1908. Soon after their release, complaints were aired that the coins were ready receptacles for dirt and would possibly help transmit disease.

Despite these concerns, Pratt's coins continued to be minted through 1929 and were no more the cause of health worries than other coins.

It was argued that the sunken designs of the Indian Head gold $2.50s and $5s would harbor germs.

★★★

In 1867, with passage paid by his father, Saint-Gaudens set out on the first of several extended stays in Europe. In Paris, while awaiting acceptance to the prestigious Ecole des Beaux-Arts, he took a position cutting cameos for a jeweler by the name of Lupi and studied at Ecole Gratuite de Dessin, where he modeled his first nude figure.

The following year he was admitted to the Ecole des Beaux-Arts, joining the atelier of Francois Jouffroy, an artist best noted for his sculpture *The Secret of Venus,* the figure of a young girl whispering into the ear of Hermes.

With the outbreak of the Franco-Prussian War, Saint-Gaudens moved to Rome and took a studio with another artist and began his marble sculpture, *Hiawatha,* the legendary Iroquois Nation chief.

In 1872 he returned to the United States, working in a studio in New York, where one of his commissions (for the Masonic Temple in New York) was *Silence,* the marble figure of a cloaked woman gesturing for silence.

He again went abroad the following year, where he met Augusta Homer of Boston, whom he would eventually marry. His stay this time was brief. Low on funds, he returned to New York in 1875 and set up a studio.

HOT TOES
Of the obverse of Adolph Weinman's popular Walking Liberty half dollar, one observer, noting the rather large sun in the background, cautioned, "Liberty in sandals taking giant strides across the face might burn her toes, if she should step one millimeter nearer the rising sun."[1]

The depiction of Liberty on the Walking Liberty half dollar was subject to criticism involving the large sun.

It was during this period that he received one of his first major commissions, a bronze statue of Civil War Navy Adm. David Farragut for Madison Square Park in New York. Two years later he married Augusta, helped found the Society of American Artists, and again set off for Europe, not returning to the United States until 1880.

★★★

President Theodore Roosevelt and sculptor Augustus Saint-Gaudens hoped to produce U.S. coins in a much higher relief.

His reputation as a master sculptor continued to grow, as did his list of commissions. Notable in a brief listing of his most memorable monuments are the *Shaw Memorial,* Boston Common, Boston; the *Puritan,* Fairmount Park, Philadelphia; *General John A. Logan Monument,* Grant Park, Chicago; *Roswell P. Flower Monument,* Watertown, N.Y.; *Adams Memorial,* Rock Creek Church Cemetery, Washington, D.C.; *Diana,* Philadelphia Museum of Art; and two figures of Lincoln — *Abraham Lincoln: The Head of State* (seated), Grant Park, and *Abraham Lincoln: The Man* (standing), Lincoln Park, both in Chicago.

In 1892 he received a commission to prepare a monument in honor of Civil War Gen. William T. Sherman for the Grand Army Plaza in New York, work on which was begun in New York, continued upon his return to Paris in 1897, and completed in the United States.[1]

In 1900 he won the Grand Prize at the Paris Exposition. Featured among his exhibits were the *General Sherman* and *Victory* of the *Sherman Monument.*

⋆★⋆

Saint-Gaudens returned to the United States in 1900, setting up a studio in Cornish, N.H.

During his long career he had many assistants and students, several of whom are familiar to coin collectors, including Adolph Weinman (Mercury dime and Walking Liberty half dollar), James Earle Fraser (Indian Head nickel, Oregon Trail half dollar), Hermon MacNeil (Standing Liberty quarter), John Flanagan (Washington quarter) and Bela Lyon Pratt (Indian Head $2.50 and $5 gold).

Early designs for the gold coinage featured the figure of Liberty with the addition of angel wings, a headdress and a shield.

Photograph by D.C. Ward.

A 'pet crime'

It was over a dinner in Washington, D.C., in the winter of 1905, that Roosevelt and Saint-Gaudens began to discuss the possibility of redesigning the nation's gold coinage. Roosevelt first became acquainted with Saint-Gaudens through the latter's

A version of Augustus Saint-Gaudens *Diana*. An 18-foot tall example served as a weathervane atop Madison Square Tower in New York.

Courtesy of Postif.

★ ★ ★

A low relief Saint-Gaudens gold $20.

appointment as a consultant to the Board of Public Buildings, working to implement the McMillan Plan (an effort to make civic improvements in the District of Columbia), and through Saint-Gaudens' labors in Washington to establish an American Academy in Rome.[2] Saint-Gaudens also designed Roosevelt's inaugural medal, the modeling for which was done by his assistant, Weinman.

Throughout the period of their acquaintance, up until Saint-Gaudens' death from cancer in 1907, the artist and the president were in regular correspondence, generally in relation to Roosevelt's "pet crime," the redesign of the nation's coinage. Thanks to the efforts of Homer Saint-Gaudens, the text of these letters have been preserved and published, showing the channels by which the $10 and $20 gold coins were remodeled in 1907.

The content of the letters has been transcribed in many numismatic sources since, but initially appeared in the April 1920 publication of "Roosevelt and Our Coin Designs: Letters Between Theodore Roosevelt and Augustus Saint-Gaudens" by *Century Illustrated Monthly Magazine.*

On Nov. 6, 1905, Roosevelt wrote to Saint-Gaudens requesting that the artist provide an update as to what progress had been made, asking, "How is that old gold coinage design getting along?"

Roosevelt suggested that it seemed worthwhile "to try for a really good coinage, though I suppose there will be a revolt about it!" Roosevelt's reference to a "good coinage" reflected his admiration for the coins of ancient Greece.

★★★

"I was looking at some gold coins of Alexander the Great today, and I was struck by their high relief," he wrote to Saint-Gaudens. "Would it not be well to have our coins in high relief, and also to have the rims raised?" The raising of the rims, he said, would protect the high-relief design from wear.[3] Saint-Gaudens responded on Nov. 11, 1905:

> You have hit the nail on the head with regard to the coinage. Of course the great coins (and you might almost say the only coins) are the Greek ones you speak of, just as the great medals are those of the fifteenth century by Pisanello and Sperandio.[4]

Saint-Gaudens said he would be pleased to undertake a redesign, but feared Mint officials would "throw fits" because of the problems with striking coins in high relief, namely the number of blows necessary to bring up the design and the inability to do so and still maintain the high-speed coinage expected of a modern mint.

LEGAL DOUBLE EAGLE

The government claims there's only one 1933 $20 gold piece that can be legally held and that is the one sold to an anonymous collector for a then record price of $7.59 million in a July 2002 auction. According to its take on this rarity, none were to have been released into circulation in 1933, the same year the Roosevelt Administration banned most private ownership of gold. However, some 1933 double eagles did escape the Mint, and there are those who argue the government's case doesn't stand up.

Over the years, a number of the coins have been confiscated, including 10 pieces sent to the Mint in 2004 by the relatives of the late Philadelphia jeweler Israel Switt, who it is believed obtained the coins in 1933.

The only specimen of the 1933 gold $20 that the government currently contends is legal to own.

★ ★ ★

Side view of Augustus Saint-Gaudens' Sherman Monument in New York.

Victory is at the lead in this view of Augustus Saint-Gaudens' Sherman Monument.

Saint-Gaudens was no neophyte when it came to these concerns. Having tangled with Mint chief engraver Charles Barber regarding his inaugural medal for Roosevelt, he was rightfully reticent about approaching the Mint on his own, telling Roosevelt that he thought there could be no objection to such coins if the rims could be raised high enough to prevent rubbing, but intimating that it was perhaps better if the inquiry came from Roosevelt, so as not to incur "the antagonistic reply from those who have the say in such matters that would certainly be made to me."[5]

Admitting that he hadn't as yet prepared any models for the coins, only sketches, Saint-Gaudens told the president he anticipated placing an eagle similar to the one used for the reverse of the Roosevelt inaugural medal on one side of the gold double eagle and, on the other, a figure of Liberty, possibly winged, "...striding energetically forward as if on a mountain top holding aloft on one arm a shield bearing the Stars and Stripes

★★★

with the word Liberty marked across the field, in the other hand, perhaps, a flaming torch. The drapery would be flowing in the breeze. My idea is to make it a *living* thing and typical of progress."[6] The figure was no doubt inspired by his *Victory* for the *Sherman Monument*, which Roosevelt admired.

The artist added that he remembered Roosevelt spoke of the possible use of a head of an Indian, but wondered if it would be "a sufficiently clear emblem of Liberty" to meet the provisions of the law.

In a Nov. 14, 1905, letter to Saint-Gaudens, Roosevelt said he would summon the Mint people and try to persuade them "that coins of the Grecian type," but

GODLESS COIN

When President Theodore Roosevelt argued in favor of leaving the motto "In God We Trust" off of U.S. gold coins in the early 1900s, there was uproar against the move, and the motto was soon restored. With the introduction of Presidential dollar coins in 2007, the defenders of the religious motto were again miffed to see it removed from the first coin, the George Washington dollar. Those who led the charge termed them "Godless coins." However, the religious motto hadn't been dropped, it had been moved to the coin's edge along with the date, mintmark and the motto "E Pluribus Unum." The true "Godless coin" (as well as dateless) came when error versions of the Washington dollar were discovered that were totally missing the required edge lettering.

with raised rim, would meet the needs of commerce. He also suggested the possibility of adding an Indian feather headdress. Roosevelt wrote:

> If we get down to bed-rock facts would the feather head-dress be any more out of keeping with the rest of Liberty than the canonical Phrygian cap which never is worn and never has been worn by any free people in the world?[7]

A little more than a week later, Saint-Gaudens wrote in agreement that an Indian headdress would be appropriate. "It should be very handsome," he told the president.[8]

On Jan. 7, 1906, Saint-Gaudens wrote to Adolph Weinman in search of an Indian headdress. About a month later he again queried Weinman, this time for angel wings.[9]

Whether or not either query has direct reference to the coinage design cannot be positively ascertained. Yet the suggestion is

✶★✶

strong, as it wasn't until late in May of that year that Saint-Gaudens reported to Roosevelt that the reverse of the double eagle was done and work was beginning on the obverse.

Early sketches depicted Liberty as a winged figure, with shield and feathered headdress. At one point, Saint-Gaudens contemplated adding the words "Justice" and "Liberty" to the shield.

ROLLING ON

Today, as they have been in past, coins are struck with the use of dies in a press that applies downward pressure on a planchet, causing it to pick up designs from the dies by force. These are done one at a time. However, in the late 1960s, the U.S. Mint tried to change this by testing a roller press created by General Motors. It was touted as being able to produce 10,000 coins per minute, as compared to 600-per-minute production from regular presses of the period. A description of the process in the September 1969 issue of *Coin Collector and Shopper* explained that: "Contrary to expectations, the two-unit device is not a massive machine. From the unwinding of coinage strip to the scrap accumulator, the entire unit occupies an overall floor space of 25 by 75 feet with 10 feet of overhead clearance.

"In operation, metal coinage strips are fed to the roller. The strip goes through an initial set of dies, coins are punched out, and another die finishes the coins on the opposite side. The metal strip is then turned over and passes through the second unit, where the remaining half is punched out."

Die life was said to be a problem with the roller press.

A view of the basic tool elements of the Philadelphia Mint's roller press.

★★★

Eventually it was decided to use a head in profile (originally planned for the cent) on the $10 gold piece. Thus, Roosevelt was able to have his feathered headdress, which replaced an olive wreath on an earlier design. The standing eagle, first contemplated for the double eagle, was adopted for the coin's reverse.

The Flying Eagle cent, 1856-1858.

A flying eagle, patterned after the obverse of James B. Longacre's Flying Eagle cent (1856-1858), was selected for the $20 gold piece's reverse. This same design was originally proposed for an anticipated redesign of the cent.

Relief too high

Due to his declining health, Saint-Gaudens gave the duty of modeling to an assistant, Henry Hering. From the start, Hering experienced problems with the Mint and, in particular, Saint-Gaudens' nemesis Charles Barber, who consistently rejected modelings as being unsuitable for high-speed modern coinage.

Hering gave a detailed vent to his feelings toward the Mint and its chief engraver in an article, "History of the $10 and $20 Gold Coins of 1907 Issue," in the August 1949 issue of *The Numismatist.*

Hering explained that due to Saint-Gaudens' ill health, he had been charged with executing the modeling of the $10 and $20 coins from Saint-Gaudens' original designs and with dealing with the Mint on a one-to-one basis.

"I proceeded to make a model in very high relief, knowing perfectly well they could not stamp it in one strike, my object being to have a die made of this model and then have strikes made in order to see the various results," Hering wrote of early work on the gold $20.[10]

He took this plaster model (measuring nearly 9 inches in diameter) to the Mint, where he was introduced to Barber. Barber rejected the model as being impossible to strike by any mint. It was only "after considerable discussion" that Barber agreed to make the die.

* * *

Hering returned to the studio and started work on a second modeling in lower relief. He was just about finished when the Mint informed him that the die of the first model was ready for experiment.

Augustus Saint-Gaudens, circa 1878.

"I immediately went to Philadelphia carrying the second and revised model with me," he wrote. "When I showed it to Mr. Barber it was no more practical than the first model and he refused to have anything to do with it."[11]

Tests were conducted with the experimental die of the first model, Hering relating that the first stamping with 172 tons of hydraulic pressure showed "a little more than one-half the modeling."

It would take until the ninth strike before the coin was brought to full detail.

"This coin I took to show to Mr. St. Gaudens, who in turn sent it to the President, and I think Mrs. Theodore Roosevelt still has it. I do not know of any more being struck, as we had finished with that die," he wrote.[12]

Hering decided to make a third model, which Barber also rejected. Ultimately, this modeling, with its relief further reduced by the Mint, would be used for the regular-issue coinage.

"Between all these events I examined the reduction of my model, which seemed to me very poor, Mr. Barber claiming it could not be done better," Hering continued.[13] Aware from his student days in Paris that a sculptor named Janvier had invented a reducing machine "which was perfection," and which had been installed in several European mints, Hering decided the Mint's problems might stem from its use of an antiquated machine.

"It was a machine about forty years old and consequently very much out of date," he wrote. "I told Mr. Barber so but it made no impression on him, so I made my report to Mr. St. Gaudens who in turn told the President. Of course you can imagine what

★★★

Teddy's feelings were on hearing the U.S.A. was so much out of date."[4] The Mint soon replaced its out-of-date Hill machine with a Janvier lathe.

It didn't help; at least it didn't help Hering. Upon his return to the Mint, Barber showed him "with great glee" a reduction of the $10 gold coin using the Janvier lathe. It was also poorly done. Hering reacted boldly, telling Barber that "a bad reduction can be made from a good machine" and suggested that maybe Barber wasn't sufficiently well acquainted with the machine to make a good reduction. Hering said he was able to make the assertion knowing full well he was right, having taken the precaution of having examples, in three different reliefs, prepared outside the Mint by a Janvier lathe.

RECYCLED DESIGNS

Good coinage designs never die, they get reused. This happened frequently in the late 20th and into the 21st century, when modifications of earlier designs began appearing on bullion coins and commemoratives. Included among the new coins with old designs are the silver American Eagle, first issued in 1986, bearing an obverse after Adolph Weinman's Walking Liberty half dollar (1916-1947); the gold American Eagle, first minted in 1986, with an obverse design after Augustus Saint-Gaudens' gold $20 (1907-1933); the 2001 American Buffalo silver dollar and American Buffalo gold $50, first minted in 2006, both with obverse and reverse designs based on James Earle Fraser's Buffalo nickel (1913-1938); and the 1999 George Washington Bicentennial gold $5 with designs by Laura Gardin Fraser first selected to appear on the Washington quarter in 1932.

The ultimate form of this flattery came in 2009 when the U.S. Mint released Augustus Saint-Gaudens' gold $20 in ultra high relief — a form the artist had hoped would prove practical for regular coinage of the design.

In 2009 the U.S. Mint recreated the Saint-Gaudens ultra high relief $20 in gold.

★★★

Saint-Gaudens' poor health, Hering writes, was likely behind the president's urging that the Mint go ahead with coinage. The Mint struck off several hundred high-relief specimens from the second modeling, which produced a wire rim and led to complaints from bankers about the inability of the coins to stack properly.

Mint engraver Charles Barber.

This, Hering charged, wouldn't have happened if the Mint had employed his third model in its original form, without the additional reduction made prior to its use for regular coinage.

Saint-Gaudens died on Aug. 3, 1907. His coins were released into circulation shortly thereafter.

Upset by the outcome of his strained negotiations with the Mint and the look of its low-relief product, Hering refused to give final approval to the designs, which meant Saint-Gaudens' widow, Augusta, could not be paid. He relented at meeting with Mint officials in the spring of 1908, succumbing to pressure from Homer Saint-Gaudens and Augusta's lawyer.

Hering said he used the meeting to explain that he hadn't approved the gold $20 because the coin in circulation was not a good reduction of his third modeling. He showed his Janvier reductions of the $10 piece as proof. This was, however, to no avail.

An Irish lass

Since the coin's release, many numismatic writers have taken on the task of relating the background of the gold double eagle.

The story that Mary Cunningham served as a model keeps coming to the forefront and is likely the most remembered by numismatists. This is perhaps because of statements by Homer Saint-Gaudens and a press dispatch from Harrisburg, Pa., dated Sept. 19, 1907.[15]

The dispatch reported that the Independent Order of Americans, which was holding its annual convention in Harrisburg, "has adopted a protest against the proposed placing of the face of Miss Mary Cunningham, the Irish-born girl, upon the United States

★★★

gold coins, and has authorized the State Councilor to forward the protest to the United States Government at Washington."

The dispatch said that Cunningham, 26, a waitress in the town of Cornish, near Windsor, Vt., was the model, explaining that Saint-Gaudens had had difficulty finding the proper model for the new coins, with "many beautiful girls rejected by him," before he found Cunningham on his summer stay in Cornish.

"She waited on him at table, and he almost immediately decided that hers was the face for the new coins," the dispatch said. Cunningham, who had come to the United States a few years prior, was reluctant, never having served as a model. "She simply let him copy her face because he was so very much in earnest."

Cunningham's "classic face," it said, was to appear on the cent, $10 gold piece and the $20 gold piece.

A cherished family story

Cunningham wasn't the only rumored model. Others have suggested it was Davida Clark, Saint-Gaudens' mistress, or Alice Butler, said by Louise Hall Harp in *Saint-Gaudens and the Guided Era* to have been the model for the profile head of the gold $10 coin. Another reference, often quickly passed over, was to the aforementioned "woman supposed to have negro blood in her veins."

It was within this comment by Homer Saint-Gaudens and an oft-told, cherished family story that truth may lay hidden.

The story that follows is the result of research by William E. Hagans, first published under his byline in the Feb. 26, 1991, issue of *Numismatic News.*

Hagans was drawn into the world of coin collecting and the background of the models for the Saint-Gaudens double eagle following the death of his mother in 1988. He and his sisters had come across an old photograph, taken in the 1890s, of a beautiful young woman.

"We recalled that this was the cousin my grandmother often spoke of, who had posed for an important statue in New York and was represented on a gold coin," Hagans wrote.[16]

Also discovered was a sack of old coins. Hagans was charged with ascertaining the value, leading him to a fruitful "crash course in numismatics."

* * *

While identifying the gold coins within the bag, Hagans said he kept coming upon references to Saint-Gaudens and his gold coin designs.

"After I found Hettie Anderson's name on our family tree and her Manhattan street number in my grandmother's old address book, it was time to pursue the Saint-Gaudens' connection," he wrote.[17]

Hagans' big break in connecting Anderson to the *Sherman Monument* and the gold coin came when he obtained a copy of *The Work of Augustus Saint-Gaudens* by John H. Dryfhout, then curator of Aspet, the Saint-Gaudens National Historical Site in Cornish, N.H. In it, Hagans found reference to Hettie Anderson (or "Cousin Tootie" as she is known within family circles) as being the first model for the head of *Victory* for Saint-Gaudens' *Sherman Monument*.

Dryfhout's heavily illustrated volume on the works of Augustus Saint-Gaudens shows a bust of Anderson by Saint-Gaudens, with Dryfhout's notation that it was the first head of *Victory,* and the one eventually employed. Inscribed on a label attached to the bust is: "First Sketch of Head/Victory/Sherman Monument" "To Hettie Anderson/AVGVSTVS Saint-Gavdens/1897."

Dryfhout adds that "Hettie Anderson was a New York model who posed for Saint-Gaudens."[18]

At the time his book was published, 1982, the whereabouts of the bust was not known.

Hagans had found his link to the important statue in New York and the gold coin told of in the old family story. Yet, he wondered, why hadn't anyone other than Dryfhout observed the connection?

According to Hagans, the answer lies in the deception of Homer Saint-Gaudens, who took charge after his father's death and, Hagans says, worked, as much as possible, to expunge from the record references to Davida Clark and obscure the possibility that an African-American served as a model for the $20 gold piece.[19]

That Homer Saint-Gaudens was aware that Anderson modeled for *Victory* is apparent from Anderson's response to a letter written by Homer Saint-Gaudens in August 1907, less than a week after his father's death, asking her to lend the bust so that a duplicate could be made.

*** *

Photograph courtesy of the Hogans Family Collection.

Hetty Anderson, first model for
Saint-Gaudens' *Victory.*

Anderson replied in January of the following year:

> I rec'd your letter of the 9th asking me to loan,
> for the purpose of duplicating, the study of the head
> made from me, by Mr. Saint-Gaudens, when he first
> began the Sherman Group. When Mr. Saint-Gaudens
> gave me the head he...said: 'Some day this may be
> valuable to you, and if you will let me I will take it
> abroad and have it put in bronze for you, it may be
> worth a great deal of money.' I thanked him, but told
> him that I thought I would take it then — which I
> did. Valuing it as I do, and knowing as I do that it is
> the only one in existence, in that state — I am not
> willing to have any duplicates made of it, for any
> purpose whatever... (Dartmouth College Library.)[20]

★

Hagans said his cousin's fear of duplication was not unfounded. A second head of *Victory* was copied in quantity and sold commercially.

According to Hagans, the price Anderson paid for not giving in was her being left out of history as the first model for the head and torso of *Victory*.

A BETTER DESIGN

Some of the best coin designs never got used. There are numerous patterns that ended up only as patterns, including the 1879 Schoolgirl dollar by George T. Morgan and the 1872 Amazonian quarter, half and dollar coins by William Barber.

George Washington could have appeared on a U.S. coin much earlier than the 1901 Lafayette dollar had an 1866 pattern bearing his likeness been chosen for the five-cent piece instead of the selected design, which was unflatteringly termed by Joseph Wharton as "a tombstone surmounted by a cross overhung by weeping willows."

Some argue Felix Schlag's original design for the reverse of the Jefferson nickel is far superior to the one adopted.

The 1879 School Girl pattern dollar by George T. Morgan.

Felix Schlag's original design for the Jefferson nickel.

★★★

Victor D. Brenner, designer of the Lincoln cent.

INITIAL CONTROVERSY

The 1909-S V.D.B. Lincoln cent is a classic in the Lincoln cent series. It is so because of the appearance of the designer's initials at the base of the coin's reverse and because the San Francisco version of this variety had the lowest mintage. The V.D.B. stood for Victor D. Brenner, who is credited with the Lincoln cent. First issues in 1909 carried his initials. That was until Treasury Secretary Franklin MacVeagh apparently objected to the prominent display of the V.D.B. and order coinage of the cent halted. New cents were minted sans the designer's initials, which didn't return to the cent until 1918 and then in an obscure location on the truncation of the Lincoln bust on the coin's obverse. The Philadelphia Mint also struck Lincoln cents with the V.D.B. on the reverse, but these are much more common. The S-mint version is a premium coin in all grades.

Victor D. Brenner's "V.D.B." initials appeared at the base of the coin's reverse on the first Lincoln cents released in 1909.

In 1913 Homer Saint-Gaudens supervised the editing of his father's memoirs, renaming it *The Reminiscences of Augustus Saint-Gaudens* (this from his father's suggested *The Reminiscences of an Idiot*), leaving out Anderson's *Victory* bust from the "complete" catalog of his father's work, despite the fact that by that time it had been bronzed and placed on display in a memorial of the sculptor's work in 1908 at New York's Metropolitan Museum of Art.[21]

Saint-Gaudens spoke glowingly of Anderson in the uncensored version of the *Idiot* memoirs. Saint-Gaudens wrote:

> I...modeled...the nude for the figure of Victory of the Sherman group, from certainly the handsomest model I have ever seen of either sex, and I have seen a great many... The model was a young woman from Georgia [actually, South Carolina, born in 1873], dark long legged, which is not common with women, and which if not exaggerated, is an essential requirement for beauty; Besides she had what is also rare with handsome models, a power of posing patiently, steadily and thoroughly in the spirit one wished. She could be depended on... Having seen her the other day for the first time in eight years, I found her just as splendid as she was fifteen years ago when she was first drawn to my attention... (Dartmouth College Library.)[22]

In February 1897 Saint-Gaudens reported to his niece, Rose Nichols, that work was progressing rapidly with his *Victory* model. He also mentioned that Swedish artist Anders Zorn had made an etching of him and of his model during a rest period.

"The etching is a beautiful representation of the obviously tired, middle-aged sculptor, his distinctive leonine features half obscured by shade, and the vibrant young model reclining nude in the background, surrounded by Zorn's swirling lines," Hagans wrote. "It has been assumed by some that the model was Davida, his mistress, but the resemblance to Hettie Anderson is unmistakable."[23]

According to Hagans, the same letter appears in Homer Saint-Gaudens' version of the memoirs, including the reference to the model, but with the substitution of a Zorn etching produced

★★★

a year later in Paris. The published etching shows Saint-Gaudens' *Puritan* statue in the background, not his model for *Victory.*

Ten years after Zorn's etchings were made, Augustus Saint-Gaudens wrote to the artist in August 1906:

Swedish artist Anders Zorn's etching of Augustus Saint-Gaudens and the model for Victory, Hettie Anderson. (New York, 1897).

Photograph courtesy of the Hagans Family Collection.

> Your masterpiece of me hangs in my study and is a constant pleasure; I wish I could really repay you for it. You know I promised you a reduction of my nude of the Goddess-like Miss Anderson, but...it was destroyed in the fire [of 1904 at Cornish]... (Zorn Collections, Mora, Sweden)[24]

Hagans said the "only veiled allusion" to Hettie Anderson made by Homer Saint-Gaudens was his mention of a woman with "negro blood in her veins." Homer Saint-Gaudens had written of the model:

> The profile head Saint-Gaudens modeled in relief from a bust originally intended for the Sherman Victory, adding the feathers upon the President's suggestion. Many persons knew it as the 'Mary Cunningham' design, because posed for by an Irish maid, when only a 'pure American' should have served for a model for our national coin. As a matter of fact, the so-called features of the Irish girl appear scarcely the size of a pinhead upon the full-length Liberty, the body of which was posed for by a Swede. Also, the modern American blue blood may delight in the discovery that the profile head was modeled from a woman supposed to have negro blood in her veins. Who other than an Indian may be a 'pure American' is undetermined.[25]

According to Hagans, although quite fair, his cousin was indeed black.

★★★

Photographs by Lawrence Chamberlain.

The bust of Hettie Anderson by Augustus Saint-Gaudens, used in preparation of his *Victory* for the *Sherman Monument*.

Additional research conducted by Hagans into the letters of Adolph Weinman led to the discovery of a highly suggestive letter written by Augustus Saint-Gaudens during the time period in which Saint-Gaudens was hard at work on the double eagle design. Dated Jan. 2, 1906, it reads:

> Dear Weinman: Will you please mail the enclosed letter to Miss Anderson. Perhaps if she is posing for you, you might let her go for one, two or three days, I need her badly...[26]

Though not conclusive, Saint-Gaudens' call for Anderson to serve again as a model is interesting in light of Homer Saint-Gaudens' claim that a Swedish woman, likely Davida Clark, served as the model for the torso.

According to Hagans, by the 1890s, Augustus Saint-Gaudens' affair with Clark and the resulting child had been discovered by the sculptor's wife, Augusta, and "Davida was exiled to Darien, Conn." Although the sculptor occasionally saw Davida and their son, Louis P. Clark, "her posing for the double eagle is highly doubtful, especially given his grave illness and the watchfulness of Augusta."[27]

Victory bust recovered

In 1990, with Dryfhout's help, the Hagans were fortunate to recover the missing *Victory* bust of Hettie Anderson. Hagans wrote:

> When my wife [Willow] and I visited the Saint-Gaudens National Historic Site in Cornish, N.H., in summer 1988, Mr. Dryfhout's first words in reference to Anderson were that he had been looking for the bust of her for the last 20 years. In his exhaustive cataloging of the sculptor's work, Hettie's bust was one of the few works whose location remained a mystery.[28]

In early 1990 Dryfhout informed Hagans that the bust had surfaced and was going on auction at Christie's in New York. Hagans and his wife purchased the bust and say, in time, they plan to donate it to the National Historic Site in New Hampshire, where the bust of Hettie Anderson can take "her rightful place among the sculptor's magnificent creations."

★★★

Chapter 9

Meeker's Coin

*T*he Oregon commemorative half dollar was once called the Ezra Meeker coin by those who promoted it. Sure, it was a stunt to sell more coins — the same design had similarly been tagged the Jedediah Smith coin, the Jason Lee coin, and the Fort Laramie coin — but the most appropriate was Meeker's name.

Trail bound

In 1906, against the advice of family and friends, Meeker, then 76, set out from his home in Puyallup, Wash., with a covered

The first Oregon Trail half dollars were minted in 1926 with a design by James Earle Fraser and Laura Gardin Fraser.

* * *

Ezra Meeker worked through much of his life to promote marking the Oregon Trail.

wagon pulled by two oxen, Dave and Dandy, and his pet dog, Jim, to retrace the 2,000 miles of the famed Oregon Trail that had led many to the West during the days of the Gold Rush. Only this time, unlike when he made the trip with his wife and 1-year-old son some 50 years earlier, he would be heading east not west.

★★★

Ezra Meeker with his dog and covered wagon.

His trip had one aim, to mark the trail that had been traveled by tens of thousands of brave pioneers seeking a better life in the years following the discovery of gold in California. Some 20,000 Americans lost their lives along the Oregon Trail. Meeker wrote that he made the 1906 trip "to honor the memories of these true heroes and kindle in the breasts of the rising generation a flame of patriotism."

Marking history

Traveling the trail eastward, Meeker stopped in towns along the way, where, with the help of townspeople, he erected markers and gave dedication speeches.

When money ran short, he printed his trail journal, calling it *The Ox Team or the Old Oregon Trail.* He sold copies for 50 cents in clothbound and 25 cents in paper back.

FIRST LIVING PERSON
Who was the first living person to appear on a U.S. coin? The most recent was Eunice Kennedy Shriver, founder of the Special Olympics. She appeared on the obverse of the 1995 Special Olympics silver dollar. The first, however, was Gov. T.E. Kilby on the 1921 Alabama Centennial half dollar.

His travels brought him to Washington, D.C., where he met with President Teddy Roosevelt and received a pledge of federal funds for permanently marking the trail.

★

FIRST COMMEM

It's sometimes called the nation's first commemorative coin and it's a coin few wouldn't want to own. The 1848 "Cal." gold $2.50 owns this distinction because it was minted from the first gold sent east following the discovery of gold in California.

In January 1848 James Marshall discovered gold along a sawmill belonging to his employer, Johann Augustus Sutter. Word soon leaked out, and less than a week later, California's military governor Col. Richard B. Mason ordered Lt. Lucien Loeser to leave for Washington, D.C., with samples of the California gold.

Loeser's samples, packed in a tea caddy, made it to the East, where they were subsequently assayed at the Philadelphia Mint and transformed into an estimated 1,389 gold $2.50s. Each coin bore a special "Cal." stamp above the eagle as recognition of the source of the gold. Few have survived, and the coin is a sought-after rarity.

To commemorate the use of the first gold from California, this 1848 gold $2.50 had a special "Cal." stamped on its reverse.

Meeker repeated portions of his trip in 1912, 1916 by auto, and 1926 by plane, but he was not done trying to commemorate the Oregon Trail. On April 26, 1926, he appeared before the Senate Committee on Banking and Currency.

Mr. Meeker goes to Washington

Now 96 years old, Meeker went before the committee as president of the Oregon Trail Memorial Association to plead for passage of Public Law 235, calling for the striking of more than 6 million Oregon Trail half dollars. He got his way. In 1926 the first Oregon Trail half dollars were sold to collectors. Designed by James Earle Fraser and his wife, Laura Gardin Fraser, the coin's obverse shows a man leading a team of oxen pulling a Conestoga wagon. Inside the wagon are the man's wife and child as they make their way to a new life, heading westward into the setting sun along the Oregon Trail. The coin's reverse has an American Indian over a map of the United States showing a line of wagons bound to the West. The brave holds a bow in his right hand, and his left arm is outstretched to the East as if to halt the white man's advance.

★

High hopes, low numbers

Although today considered one of the more attractive coins ever minted, Meeker's half dollar didn't sell as well as he hoped. 1926 saw a combined mintage from Philadelphia and San Francisco of a little more than 131,000 Oregon Trail half dollars. Aside from the 1926 coins, Oregon Trail half dollars were minted in smaller numbers in seven other years, with 1939 serving as the end.

Ezra Meeker, who dedicated most of his later years to the memory of this important trail west, died in 1928 at the age of 98. He lived to see more than 150 monuments erected along the trail. His ox team, Dave and Dandy, have been preserved and are on display at the Washington State Historical Museum in Tacoma. His mansion in Puyallup, Wash., can also be visited.

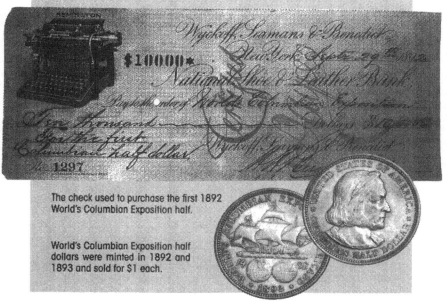

$10,000 HALF

At the time, it was not only the first commemorative half dollar, it was also the first one to sell for $10,000. In 1892 Remington Typewriter Co. paid that amount for the first (actually second) 1892 World's Columbian Exposition half dollar struck, as a promotional stunt. The World's Columbian Exposition half dollars were minted in 1892 and 1893 and initially sold to the public at $1 per coin.

$10000*

1297

The check used to purchase the first 1892 World's Columbian Exposition half.

World's Columbian Exposition half dollars were minted in 1892 and 1893 and sold for $1 each.

★★★

FINALLY BRONZED

It took 65 years after the commemorative half dollar depicting it was struck before the *Pioneer Memorial* by sculptor Trygve Rovelstad was dedicated along the banks of the Fox River in Elgin, Ill., on July 4, 2001. For much of the time prior to that the 12-foot high grouping of four pioneers engulfed an Elgin home/studio, awaiting funding for a bronze version to be erected.

The Elgin half dollar, released in 1936, shows the four figures relating to the founding of Elgin as they appear in the planned memorial, hopes for which were dashed until 2001, years after Rovelstad and his wife had passed.

For many years Trygve Rovelstad's epic *Pioneer Memorial* remained in his Elgin, Ill., home and studio. Shown here is a portion of the grouping prior to bronzing, along with the 1936 Elgin half dollar.

Chapter 10

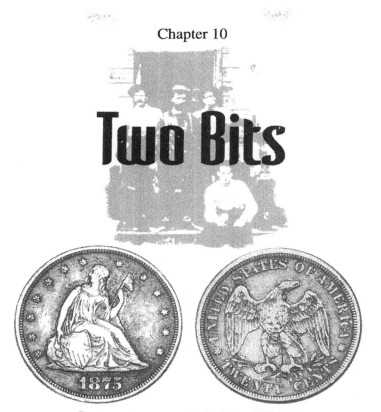

Twenty-cent pieces were minted only from 1875-1878.

One of the more interesting stories about the short-lived U.S. 20-cent piece — coined from 1875-1878 — can be found in a classic 1876 book related to Virginia City, Nev.'s Comstock Lode. It's titled *The Big Bonanza* and was written by Dan De Quille (William Wright), editor of the Virginia City *Territorial Enterprise*.

The 20-cent piece was produced for use primarily in the West, where small change was in short supply. Its chief backer was Nevada Sen. John Percival Jones, a veteran of the Comstock, and it received support from those few who advocated a metric coinage system and others who thought the coin might help absorb some of the oversupply of silver then weighing down the country.

★★★

The 1876-CC 20-cent piece is a rarity. Few exist in any grade.

That it would be of some use, at least in Western saloons, was clearly shown by De Quille. In his chapter, "Saloon Birds," De Quille explained that Virginia City had about 100 saloons, most of which were what were called "bit" houses, where "...drinks of all kinds and cigars are one bit — twelve and one half cents. The dime, however, passes as a 'bit' in all of these houses."

Being short of 12 1/2 cents, De Quille explained, it was sometimes referred to as a "short bit," but was still considered the equal of half of the quarter. Thus, in a bit house, whenever a customer tendered a quarter for his cigar or drink, he got back a dime, losing five cents in the transaction. Jones' 20-cent piece, De Quille assured, would cure this ill.

It wasn't a problem in the two-bit houses, as everything there went for a quarter (even that which sold in the bit houses for 10 cents, including beer, soda water and lemonade). However, in some cases, ambiance was apparently all you were getting in choosing the two-bit house over the one-bit house, as evidenced by the following passage from *The Big Bonanza:*

"A man one day sauntered into a two-bit saloon and called for drink of whisky. The proprietor of the place was behind the bar and set out the bourbon bottle. When the man had drunk he threw a ten-cent piece on the counter and started off.

"'This is a two-bit house, sir,' said the proprietor in a tone which showed that he felt pride in the establishment.

"'Ah!' said the customer. 'Two-bit house, eh? Well, I thought so when I first came in, but after I had tasted your whisky I concluded it was a bit house.'"

★★★

ISABELLA AND LAFAYETTE

Who was the first foreign ruler to appear on a U.S. coin? It was Queen Isabella of Spain, who is shown on the 1893 Isabella commemorative quarter. The coin, issued in conjunction with the World's Columbian Exposition being held in Chicago that year, was the result of efforts by the Board of Lady Managers, headed by Chicago socialite Mrs. Potter Palmer. The design, by Charles Barber, has Queen Isabella on the obverse and a female on the reverse with a distaff and spindle — said to represent women's industry.

A popular collectible today, these quarters were initially sold at $1 each.

In 1900 the head of Marquis de Lafayette of France appeared on the first U.S. commemorative dollar along with George Washington. The coin's reverse has Lafayette on horseback and is similar to a statue in Paris given to France by the United States. Lafayette played a key military role for the Continental Army in the American Revolution.

The coins were initially offered at $2 each.

Queen Isabella of Spain, 1599.

The 1893 Isabella quarter.

WEAK LINK

Placement of a design of linked rings (likely representing the unity of the Colonies as a new nation) on the reverse of the first coinage of large cents in 1793 was deemed improper. It was termed by one newspaper as a "bad omen of liberty." The design was quickly replaced.

The initial 1793 cent with its chain reverse.

Despite its importance to those who populated Virginia City's at times raucous drinking establishments, the 20-cent piece was not popular with much of the rest of the public. Being too close in size and design to the 25-cent piece, it was often confused and therefore shunned. Coinage ended in 1878, two short years, or a bit, after it began.

★★★

Chapter 11

formidable
Presence

The Anthony dollar never really caught on with the public.

*M*ost Americans never warmed up to the Susan B. Anthony dollar (1979-1999). Most argued it was too close in size to a quarter and caused confusion (something that happened in the 1800s with the short-lived 20-cent piece). Others just didn't like the design. Anthony, though honored for being a leader of the woman's suffrage movement, doesn't necessarily make for a beloved coinage design — many realistic portraits don't. Chief Mint engraver Frank Gasparro's Anthony compares favorably to a picture of her earlier in life, but the period clothing and hairstyle harshened the image.

★★*

Actually, Gasparro wanted another design of his to grace the mini-dollar — one showing a flowing hair Liberty on the obverse (reminiscent of early 19th-century designs) and an eagle in flight on the coin's reverse.

Lesser known is that, though Anthony received considerable support among women's groups for her placement on the coin (including, likely, from grand niece Dr. Susan B. Anthony, also a feminist, who was 63 when the coin was issued), some were not happy. They protested the release of the coin as being a bid to "'co-opt the women's movement' and divert public attention from pressing problems affecting American women that haven't yet been addressed,'" reported the July 14, 1979, issue of *Numismatic News*. Picketing outside of the Susan B. Anthony House in

SIT PRETTY

Just as the unverified story goes that George and Martha Washington provided silver plate for the nation's first coinage, so it is said that Martha Washington posed for the design on the 1792 half disme. It's a tradition pretty well disputed today but one of those romantic tales many probably wish were true.

An old rumor had it that Martha Washington was the subject for the 1792 half disme.

The famed 1792 half disme. The spelling of dime here is original to the period.

★★★

Anthony dollar designer Frank Gasparro.

The various stages of production leading to the final Anthony dollar design.

Susan B. Anthony.

Susan B. Anthony's home in Rochester, N.Y., is now a National Historic Landmark.

A suffrage march. Women were granted the right to vote through passage of the 19th Amendment, which became part of the Constitution in 1920.

Rochester, N.Y., where U.S. Mint Director Stella B. Hackel was holding a news conference introducing the new coin, one of the protesters, who were there arguing for better preservation of the documents and photographs maintained at the historic home, carried a sign noting "Women will not be bought off by a coin."

Though only five-foot-four in height, Anthony was a formidable presence in her day. In 1873 she was tried and found guilty of voting illegally in the 1872 presidential election after having cast her ballot in Rochester's 8th ward. She died in 1906, 14 years before the 19th Amendment for woman's suffrage was implemented.

★★★

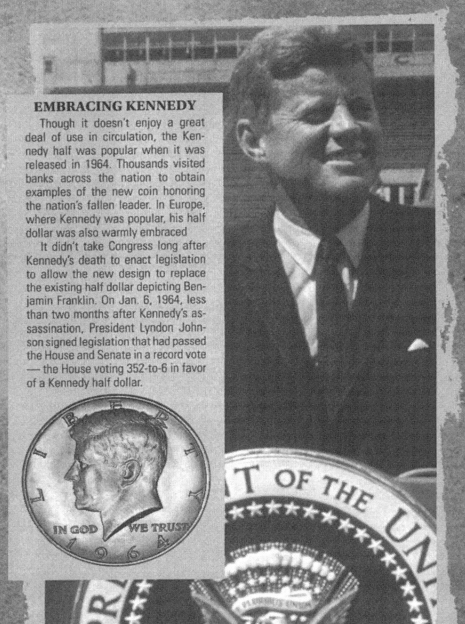

EMBRACING KENNEDY

Though it doesn't enjoy a great deal of use in circulation, the Kennedy half was popular when it was released in 1964. Thousands visited banks across the nation to obtain examples of the new coin honoring the nation's fallen leader. In Europe, where Kennedy was popular, his half dollar was also warmly embraced

It didn't take Congress long after Kennedy's death to enact legislation to allow the new design to replace the existing half dollar depicting Benjamin Franklin. On Jan. 6, 1964, less than two months after Kennedy's assassination, President Lyndon Johnson signed legislation that had passed the House and Senate in a record vote — the House voting 352-to-6 in favor of a Kennedy half dollar.

Congress moved quickly following the assassination of President John F. Kennedy to place his image on the half dollar.

Chapter 12

It's Not a Penny

Don't call a "cent" a "penny."

Some people get all wound up over proper and improper use of words and terminology. Others don't really care. Numismatists, as a whole, likely fall into the former category. Just call a U.S. cent a penny, even in casual conversation, and watch the fur fly.

Numismatists are a proud bunch — especially when it comes to their specialized knowledge.

Is it more accurately described as an Indian Head nickel or a Buffalo nickel? Is it a Mercury dime or a Winged Liberty dime? How about Christian Gobrecht's famous Liberty for the coins of the mid-1800s? Are the coins better described as Seated Liberty or Liberty Seated?

Get on the wrong side of any of these and you're likely to raise a long-winded debate as to what history shows as the proper usage.

★★★

Is it better to say "Seated Liberty" or "Liberty Seated"?

This trait is nothing new to collectors of U.S. coins. For example, collectors were quick to point out that the buffalo on the 1913-1938 nickel is more accurately termed a bison (yet they continue to call the coin a Buffalo nickel).

They take pride in telling that the figure on the obverse of Adolph Weinman's dime is not really that of the Roman god Mercury. Rather, it's Liberty with wings attached to her cap. The wings symbolize "liberty of thought."

Then there's the fact that there is three times as much copper in the U.S. five-cent piece than nickel, yet the public persists in calling the coin a nickel. Actually, most would probably be surprised to know that, because of its nickel content, the first Flying Eagle cents were called nickels in their day. That is, when they weren't being referred to as "buzzard cents."[1]

There's nothing really wrong with all of this. It's part of the fun of the hobby.

Back in the early 1900s it was common for dimes, quarters and half dollars to be called "Morgans." This carried over to later coin albums, which spread the incorrect usage.

Any numismatist worth his salt knows that George T. Morgan designed the dollar (1878-1921), not the dime (1892-1916), quarter (1892-1916), and half dollar (1892-1915). Those coins were by Charles E. Barber and are correctly known today as Barber dimes, quarters and half dollars. Yet there are probably some old-time numismatists out there still calling these coins Morgans.

★★★

POORER STILL

Coin grading is subjective. One person might view a given coin as grading Very Fine and another jump its grade to Extremely Fine. This is evidenced by the popularity of third-party grading firms, which for a fee will independently grade and encapsulate a coin.

However, no one can doubt the honesty displayed by Bangs, Mervin & Co. in its Dec. 17, 1869, auction of the J.M. Wilbur collection. Of the some 60 large cents offered for sale, the highest grade of any was "barely fair." Others were "poor," "poorer," "worse," "extremely poor," "unusually poor," "wretchedly poor," "still worse," "exceedingly poor," and "poorer still."

Grading is subjective.

SPECIAL MINT SETS

The existence of Special Mint Sets still sometimes confuses those encountering them in collections. Due to a coinage shortage in the mid-1960s, and an unwarranted fear that collectors were the cause of it, the Treasury stepped back from issuing proof sets to focus on circulating coinage.

So, instead of releasing annual proof sets, the Treasury announced that the San Francisco Mint would issue Special Mint Sets. Unlike proof sets, which were of higher quality, the Treasury said the new collector sets (including the annual cent, nickel, dime, quarter and half dollar) would "be struck one at a time from specially prepared blanks, on high tonnage presses and handled individually after striking. They will have a higher relief than regular coins and be better in appearance than any of the regular uncirculated sets heretofore issued."

The sets were sold at $4 each, and like the circulating coinage at the time, carried no mintmarks. Special Mint Sets were issued from 1965-1967. Proof sets returned in 1968.

DON'T DRINK AND CLEAN

Don't drink and clean your coins. Actually, it's best not to clean coins in the first place. It's too easy to damage a coin, resulting in an unnatural color or miniscule scratches that can be seen under magnification and lower the coin's value.

However, coin cleaning has not always been taboo. And in one case this led to the death of a prominent numismatist.

It all happened on June 24, 1922. World-renowned numismatist J. Sanford Saltus was discovered in his room at London's Hotel Metropole, lying on the floor, fully dressed. He was dead at age 69, but not from natural causes.

A coroner's jury labeled Saltus' passing as "death by misadventure," according to an account in the August 1922 issue of the American Numismatic Association's publication, *The Numismatist.*

The day prior to his death, Saltus bought a small quantity of potassium cyanide for use in cleaning silver coins he had just purchased. Although a deadly poison, collectors in those days sometimes used it. Unfortunately, at some point after Saltus retired to his room, he ordered a bottle of ginger ale. "A glass containing the poison and another glass containing ginger

ale were found side by side on the dressing table," *The Numismatist* reported, "and it is believed that while interested in cleaning the coins he took a drink of the poison in mistake for the ginger ale."

At the time, Saltus, who hailed from the United States, was president of the British Numismatic Society as well as one of the major benefactors of the American Numismatic Society. A prestigious award for medallic art is still presented each year in his honor by the ANS.

J. Sanford Saltus was one of the top numismatists of his day. Today a prestigious award continues to be presented in his honor.

Chapter 13

Million Dollar Exhibit

Have you ever seen 1 million silver dollars? Well, you could have, if you attended the 1962 Seattle World's Fair. Three Washington numismatists were behind bringing the coins to the fair. The problem was obtaining that many silver dollars, how to transport the coins, and how to display them. The three, who had formed Northwest Historic Medals Inc., were able to convince Behlen Manufacturing Co., Columbus, Neb., to build a storage facility at the fair as a promotion for the company, which manufactured steel buildings. They then arranged to borrow the silver dollars from the Philadelphia Mint in return for an interest payment.

★★★

Entry to the display of the $1 million silver dollars at the Seattle World's Fair.

★★★

The trucks that transported the 1 million silver dollars to the Seattle World's Fair in 1962.

While details were being worked out on shipping the coins, and construction began on the building in which to hold them, Northwest went about designing and striking the medals, including a new one honoring the "Million Silver Dollars Exhibit."

The corncrib holding the 1 million silver dollars.

The fair's opening date was April 21, 1962, and Behlen worked quickly to construct the corrugated steel building, while two Chevrolet diesels were employed to carry 500,000 each of the silver dollars, still in mint-sealed bags, from the Philadelphia Mint to the fair.

★★★

Once at the fair, 800,000 of the coins (Morgan dollars, apparently, as the bags were sealed between 1910 and 1915) were stacked in the center of a Behlen corncrib enclosed in glass. Then, over and around, were poured 200,000 Peace silver dollars. In June, when the 1 millionth fair visitor, a California resident, walked into the exhibit, she was presented with 100 of the silver dollars from the exhibit.

Most of the coins were likely Morgan dollars.

1964 PEACE DOLLAR?

Does a 1964-dated Peace dollar still exist? It's a question many collectors would like answered.

Coinage of the Peace dollar ended in 1935 and there had been no coins of this denomination in the intervening period minted for circulation. That was until 1964 when President Lyndon Johnson signed a law authorizing the coining of 45 million silver dollars that were to carry the Peace dollar's design.

Treasury Secretary Dillon said of the need for the new coin:

...I want you to know that the administration feels it important to continue the use of the silver dollar, as it is one of the six standard coins prescribed by law, and is particularly used as an ordinary and traditional medium of exchange in many Far Western States. Also, use of the silver dollar will, to a great extent in the West at least, alleviate the heavy demands we have had on the quarter and 50-cent pieces. This eventually will about balance out the use of silver, as the minting of halves and quarters to substitute for the 45 million silver dollars will take almost as much metal for the same end use.

The coins were to be minted at the Denver Mint, but 1964 proved to be the last year for coinage of 90-percent silver coins (the half dollar would be struck in 40 percent silver into 1970). The 316,076 1964-D Peace dollars minted were supposedly all melted, though rumors continue to suggest otherwise.

A mock-up of what a 1964 Peace dollar would look like.

★★★

LINE'S BIZZAY!

Some thought the Peace dollar's obverse, modeled after Anthony de Francisci's wife, Teresa, made Liberty look like one of that era's flappers. They termed the coin the "flapper dollar."

The *Wall Street Journal* quipped: "If words were issuing from her lips they would hardly take the more elegant languor of 'Line's bizzay!' They would more probably be, 'Say, lissen!'"[1]

The paper called for the coin's redesign, saying, "the whole thing is bad." It suggested the Peace dollar be withdrawn from circulation and a new design commissioned through a nationwide competition "It's not too much to hope that we can at least evolve something artistically above the level of the magazine cover," *the Journal* lamented.[2]

Despite this criticism, the Peace dollar continued to be coined until 1935, long after the last flapper donned her "glad rags" for a night out.

The obverse of the Peace dollar received some flack.

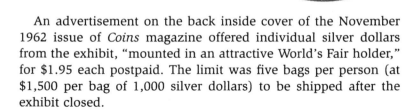

An advertisement on the back inside cover of the November 1962 issue of *Coins* magazine offered individual silver dollars from the exhibit, "mounted in an attractive World's Fair holder," for $1.95 each postpaid. The limit was five bags per person (at $1,500 per bag of 1,000 silver dollars) to be shipped after the exhibit closed.

★★★

LADY LIBERTY

Teresa de Francisci, an immigrant from Italy who arrived in America at the age of 4, liked posing as Lady Liberty as a child. Years later, she got her chance to do that for her husband, as he prepared the obverse design for the Peace silver dollar issued from 1921-1935. World War I had ended and some argued that a coin should honor the end of the war and commitment to peace.

Anthony de Francisci, with his wife as a model, created a Liberty wearing a tiara of sun rays. On the reverse, situated on the mountain on which the eagle is perched, is the word "peace."

Teresa de Francisci, who served as the model of Liberty for the Peace dollar.

Chapter 14

On a sweltering San Francisco afternoon in late August 1875, more than two years after the so-called "Crime of 1873" had been committed, a portly, middle-aged man went for his regular swim at San Francisco's North Beach, thrashing out toward Alcatraz Island. Playfully alternating between diving and floating on his back, the man swam out yards farther than most of the Neptune Bath House's regular patrons. Yet this was not unusual. He had done so many times before, as it no doubt helped to shed the day's tensions. Only this day would be different, much different. This was no ordinary man; this would be no ordinary swim.

William C. Ralston, who headed the powerful Bank of California.

★★★

The death scene. The Neptune Bath House is in the foreground.

William Chapman Ralston, once the most powerful, influential and ambitious man in California, a man who some credit with building the Golden State, and who coin collectors, economists and historians need to recognize for his great impact on 19th-century coinage laws and the nation's economy, died that day.

Some said he drowned. Some said the day's overbearing heat, combined with great personal stress and exertion, hurried the failure of an already fragile heart. Others, looking to read into the tragedy an element of human foible, eagerly pointed to Ralston's recently decimated personal fortunes, the collapse of his beloved Bank of California and his forced resignation as its president, only a few short hours prior to his death, to suggest he committed suicide. He drank a vial of poison before entering the water, gasped the worst of San Francisco's scandal-mongering early tabloids.

In the great scope of things, however, it matters not a whit how he died. Either way, one of California's most influential was lost. Either way, it was the beginning of the end of an era in which great fortunes were quickly amassed and just as quickly lost in battles waged over control of the nation's mineral wealth.

★★★

The imposing Bank of California as it once looked.

It was the end of a time characterized by ill-advised commercial ventures, questionable management decisions and overextended credit that led a once powerful institution and its popular leader to financial ruin. For, even before Ralston's motionless body was reclaimed from the chilly waters of San Francisco Bay, the tide had turned against this man and his untethered ambitions.

The world was changing. The way it viewed and handled money was changing. Ralston's place in it was all but gone. Yet aftershocks of this early empire builder's far-reaching influence would reverberate through the remainder of the century, manifested in the emotion-laden Free Silver Movement, which enjoyed great political success with its popular cry for the free and unlimited coinage of silver.

It is only through a complete look at the events that surrounded this period — which encompassed the recodification of the nation's coinage laws in 1873 and ended in an insipid whimper with William Jennings Bryan's unsuccessful bid for the presidency in 1896 — that we can truly understand the history of this tumultuous period in American history and appreciate the significance of the coins that now hold revered places in museums and numismatic collections, and in hoards of coins handed down from generation to generation. From the passage

★

William C. Ralston had his hands in many businesses as is shown in this memorial printing. The Bank of California is below his picture. At upper left is the Palace Hotel, which he didn't live to see completed.

of the Bland-Allison Act in 1878, requiring the government to inflate the nation's money supply on the heals of a partial victory for the still awakening forces of free silver through the Sherman Silver Purchase Act of 1890, which added to the heap of gleaming silver dollars languishing in Treasury vaults, the battle between monometallists and bimetallists waged in the halls of Congress and the pages of the popular press, in truth, was spawned in secret dealings between a powerful California banker and a corruptible Treasury representative during the heyday of their influence — long before the Coinage Act of 1873 was forever tagged the "Crime of 1873."

Early bonds

Under Ralston's leadership, the Bank of California had been a mainstay on the Comstock Lode (the largest silver and gold strike in U.S. history) since shortly after the lode's discovery in 1859. By the late 1860s, the "bank ring" or "bank crowd," as Ralston and his associates became known, owned or controlled most of the lode's mines, most of its ore-processing mills, and its railroad, the Virginia and Truckee.

★

H.R. Linderman, who became the first director of the Bureau of the Mint with the passage of the Coinage Act of 1873.

★★★

William C. Ralston was behind the creation of the Virginia and Truckee Railroad in Nevada, which ran from Virginia City through Gold Hill, Silver City and Carson City. In 1872, the connection was made to Reno and the Central Pacific.

Once processed, much of the Comstock ore was shipped to San Francisco, where the bank-run San Francisco Assaying and Refining Co. would refine the metal prior to its delivery at the San Francisco Mint to be turned into S-mintmarked coins. The lucrative contract had been obtained by Ralston after years of contentious lobbying in Washington and threatened, under terms of a prior act of Congress, to expire with the completion of the new San Francisco Mint at Fifth and Mission streets.

The new coinage act — a major overhaul of the nation's antiquated coinage laws — being formulated in Washington by Deputy Comptroller of the Currency John Jay Knox Jr., with former Philadelphia Mint Director Henry R. Linderman's assistance, offered Ralston opportunities to exploit the nation's need for precious metals while assuring his and the bank's continued dominance in this arena.

Just when Linderman (who had served as Philadelphia Mint director from 1867-1869) came under Ralston's influence and pay is uncertain. Documents show that by the late 1860s they were in contact and that over the next several years, Linderman accepted

★★★

At one time William C. Ralston controlled much of the Comstock Lode.

as much as $8,500 in payments from the powerful California banker.

They would become fast friends, who shared similar philosophies when it came to money matters. Both, for instance, favored a gold standard for the nation. Silver would be subsidiary. Bimetallism had worked in spits and spurts since 1792 — often with only one metal in circulation as the dearer of the two was hoarded or shipped abroad.

Linderman had been advocating for the switch to gold in his reports since the 1860s. Ralston had been influential in California's allegiance to gold payments during the Civil War and was credited with maintaining the state's prosperity while the rest of the nation yearned for the resumption of specie payments cut off with the Civil War, and suffered under the burden of depreciated paper substitutes.

Both believed in "free gold." Bankers and bullion dealers on the Pacific coast were united in their view that the U.S. Mint's half-percent charge on coining gold, in effect since 1853, was one of the primary reasons gold flowed out of this bullion-rich region to Europe and, in particular, to London. By 1869, Linderman had also signed on to the fight to eliminate the coinage charge.

★★★

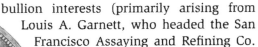

The early influence on the coinage measure by Pacific coast bullion interests (primarily arising from Louis A. Garnett, who headed the San Francisco Assaying and Refining Co. for Ralston) is shown in Knox's report accompanying the mint bill. The bill, as submitted to Congress, dropped the charge all together.

The Senate Finance Committee, becoming the focus of a vociferous debate on the Senate floor in early January 1871, would later tack on a three-tenths percent charge. Linderman was able to get the charge reduced to one-fifth percent with the passage of the Coinage Act of 1873 and totally eliminated by the Specie Resumption Act of 1875.

Both also favored private refining of government gold. Ralston had obvious reason for doing so. The new coinage act contained a provision that assured the San Francisco Assaying and Refining Co. would continue to enjoy its healthy government contract

There wasn't much call for silver dollars when coinage was ended in 1873.

beyond the completion of the new mint building in San Francisco and, according to some of his competitors, extended the bank's monopoly of influence at the San Francisco branch mint, and in turn its control over the nation's mineral wealth.

Linderman's reasons for favoring private refining were less vested. Private refineries in California, due to their advanced processes, continued to have the edge over the majority of the government refining facilities, producing a purer bar at a lower cost, with less waste.

Both likely also favored elimination of the full legal tender 412.5-grain silver dollar. Linderman certainly did, as is confirmed by his writings and recommendations to Knox concerning the mint bill. It's probable Ralston also didn't care about its continued coinage. The coin, being lighter in weight and lacking the

★★★

The Mexican eight reales had a long history of use and acceptance in China.

acceptance enjoyed by the Mexican dollar, was of no use in the bank's burgeoning trade with China. It was seen as a hindrance by many involved in such trade.

In fact, the bill as submitted to Congress didn't include the silver dollar — Knox, in his report accompanying the measure, recommended that if a dollar coin should be deemed necessary that it be in the form of a commercial dollar "of the exact value of the Mexican dollar," which "is the favorite for circulation in China and Japan and other Oriental countries."

By mid-1872, when it became apparent to Ralston and Linderman that silver was likely to fall in value (due largely to Germany's recent demonetization of that metal), they worked together on a solution that would allow the switch to a gold standard, while creating additional markets for silver. In a May 19, 1872, letter to Ralston, Linderman warned that those countries maintaining the double standard (bimetallism) would soon be overrun by silver and that, unless a home for some $50 million in silver could be found in the United States, a serious decline in price, within the next three years, was inevitable. "And this we must prevent by timely agitation & proper measures," he wrote to Ralston.

Treasury Secretary George S. Boutwell, who told Congress in a December 1872 report that silver was likely to fall in value.

On Nov. 19, 1872, parroting much of what he told Ralston in May concerning the future of silver, Linderman recommended the creation of a 420-grain "Silver Union" dollar for use in trade

★★★

In 1873, through the backing of William C. Ralston and Henry R. Linderman, the Trade dollar was minted for use in trade with the Orient.

with China, as part of his *Special Report of Examination of the Branch Mints on the Pacific Coast* to Treasury Secretary George S. Boutwell.

The idea for the new coin, Linderman told Boutwell, came about through discussions he had with gentlemen on the Pacific coast in the fall of 1872, while he was there on Treasury business. A key surviving letter to Ralston shows that by the month prior to Linderman's report, Ralston (likely at Linderman's urging) had already written to one of his correspondents in Japan to test the waters as to whether such a coin would win acceptance in the Far East.

Less than two weeks after Linderman's submission, the Treasury secretary informed Congress of the likely downturn in silver, as part of his annual report, recommending that silver only be coined for export in the form of a new trade coin as heavy as the Mexican dollar. With the passage of the Coinage Act of 1873, the Trade dollar's coinage was authorized.

In the years following, Ralston became such a heavy promoter of the coin, urging his wide-ranging contacts in Japan and China to find methods to secure the coin's official adoption, that at least one of his correspondents began calling the new trade coins "Ralston dollars."

Aside from their shared philosophies, there was another benefit to Ralston in nurturing his friendship with the former Mint director. Linderman could provide access and influence

★★★

The forces favoring the restoration of the full legal tender silver dollar to circulation got part of what they wanted with the passage of the Bland-Allison Act of 1878, leading to the coining of the Morgan dollar.

★★★

ARROWS AND RAYS

Two times in the nation's history have arrows appeared next to the date of circulation issues. The first occurred in 1853. When faced with a shortage of minor silver coins in circulation, Congress authorized lowering the weight of the half dime, dime, quarter and half dollar slightly in an attempt to keep the coins from being hoarded, melted or shipped abroad. To allow easy distinction between the heavier coins (including some dated 1853) and the lighter coins, arrows were placed at each side of the date. For the half dime and dime, arrows were used from 1853-1855. For the quarter and half dollar, the 1853 coins not only show arrows at the date, but also have rays around the eagle on the coin's reverse. For the 1854-1855 coinage of these two denominations, the rays were dropped but the arrows were maintained.

In 1873 arrows again returned to U.S. coins. The passage of the Coinage Act of 1873 mandated a slight increase in the weight of the minor silver coins to bring them in line with proposed metric coinage systems then popular. The half dime had been dropped by the coinage act, but the dime, quarter and half dollar all had arrows next to the date for the 1873 and 1874 coinage.

Of note is that these changes were not flawless. Thus, some "no arrows" coins from a given year are scarce or rare. The 1853-O "no arrows" half dime is a premium coin as is the 1853 "no arrows" quarter, and the 1853-O "no arrows" half dollar is a classic rarity with few examples known. Among the 1873 coinage, the 1873-CC "no arrows" dime is currently unique, only a handful of the 1873-CC "no arrows" quarters are known, and the 1873-CC "no arrows" half dollar is not known to exist.

The arrows and rays on this half dollar represented a slight increase in the coin's weight.

★★★

within key congressional hearings in Washington far beyond the services provided by Ralston's normal lobbyists.

Although Linderman had lost his position as director of the Philadelphia Mint in 1869, having been replaced by the Grant Administration, he continued to take regular assignments for the U.S. Treasury, under Treasury Secretary Boutwell's direction, throughout the period leading up to the Feb. 12, 1873, passage of the Coinage Act of 1873.

In the late 1860s, for example, he assisted Knox in examination of the New York Assay Office and the San Francisco Mint. By 1870, if not earlier, he was involved with Knox in co-authoring the mint bill that became the Coinage Act of 1873, at Boutwell's instigation.

In 1871, on assignment from the Treasury, he traveled to Europe to study foreign coinage systems, and in 1872 he began overseeing the installation of a refinery at the new San Francisco Mint.

Thus, within the halls of Congress, whether or not he was on current assignment from the Treasury, he was clearly considered one of its representatives, and his pronouncements in relation to coinage matters carried considerable weight. Plus, he was the leading candidate to take over the Bureau of the Mint, a position being created by the mint bill and one he would assume in 1873.

Had his compensated relationship with Ralston become known, it could have scuttled the coinage measure and placed Grant's

VALUABLE CORNERSTONE

Records indicate one 1870-S $3 gold coin was struck for inclusion in the cornerstone of the San Francisco Mint building (the Granite Lady). Yet, in 1911, a genuine 1870-S $3 gold coin appeared for sale in an offering by dealer William Woodin.

Some speculate it's a duplicate and that an additional example remains secreted among the relics within the Old Mint's cornerstone. Others believe the Woodin sale piece is the only example. No one knows for certain.

Only one example of the 1870-S gold $3 is known.

★★★

138 ★ *Fascinating* **Facts, Mysteries and Myths** *About U.S. Coins*

STELLA!

No, it's not from "A Street Car Named Desire" with Marlon Brando, but the common name given by collectors to a pattern $4 coin that showed a star on its reverse. Long before Europe's experiments with the euro, several international monetary conferences, in the latter half of the 19th century, contemplated a common standard for coinage that would allow participating nations' coins to flow across boarders at like values. The Stella, dated 1879 and 1880 in Flowing Hair and Coiled Hair versions, was the United States' effort and was brainchild of John A. Kasson, U.S. minister to Austria.

An 1879 Flowing Hair Stella. The coin also came in a Coiled Hair version.

Treasury in a tenuous position. This is likely one of the reasons Linderman sometimes used aliases on his letters to Ralston and marked most "Confidential." It also likely contributed to the fact that the payments he received from Ralston have remained so well hidden and his close involvement in the Coinage Act of 1873 largely unknown until the publication of *Crime of 1873: The Comstock Connection* by this writer in 2001.

From 1870 to 1873, Linderman accepted at least $8,500 in payments for such Coinage Act of 1873-related services as working toward having the coinage charge eliminated; assuring the continuation of Ralston's refining contract; and the introduction of the Trade dollar into the mint bill. An additional $1,500 was requested by Linderman to cover expenses, and was likely paid. In terms of today's money, the total was roughly equivalent to $167,000.

Linderman continued to act on Ralston's behalf in similar matters in later years, after he took over as Mint director under the

★★★

BAD MONEY

Ever hear of Gresham's Law? It's the name given to an observation made by 16th-century English financier Sir Thomas Gresham that, when two coins with the same face value but with differing intrinsic value are in circulation at the same time, the one with the lesser intrinsic value (bad money) will remain in circulation while the other (good money) is hoarded.

Several times throughout U.S. history, the rise and fall in the value of precious metals played havoc on its circulating coinage. When gold was dearer, it couldn't stay in circulation. When silver was more valued than gold, it disappeared through hoarding, shipment abroad or melting.

As an illustration, in 1965, when the government stopped producing 90-percent silver dimes, quarters and halves, these coins disappeared from circulation. Dimes and quarters in base metal (bad money) took their place. The half dollar continued to be minted in 40-cent silver until 1970, after which it was only produced for circulation in base metal. Today very few silver 90-percent coins (good money) are found in change.

With fluctuations in metals prices, it was often hard to keep coins in circulation.

★★★

Coinage Act of 1873, although documentation of any additional compensation is so far lacking.

The Linderman-to-Ralston letters (slightly more than one dozen in number), when weaved together with a careful analysis of the measure's history, present a clear indication that, while there wasn't any foreign intrigue in the passage of this important legislation (as promoted by late 19th-century free silver writers), not everything was aboveboard with the bill's movement through Congress.

On the wrong track

However, since 1876, by which time silver had begun to fall drastically in value, leading to the first public outcry against the Coinage Act of 1873, historians have struggled with the question of how the full legal-tender 412.5-grain silver dollar came to be dropped from the coinage measure without the silver-producing interests or their representatives in Congress protesting against its removal.

Encouraged by the often-less-than-truthful testimony of the congressmen who had voted overwhelmingly for the measure and later found themselves faced with trying to explain their actions, most writers had decided the silver-producing interests weren't paying close attention to the bill's contents as it passed through Congress or were sufficiently disinterested in a revision of the nation's coinage laws that they overlooked the change in monetary standards and the loss of their beloved silver dollar.

PLUMMETING VALUES

Not all U.S. coins continually go up in value. It's always a matter of supply and demand. This point was driven home in the early 1960s when the Treasury made a Christmas-time release of some previously rare silver dollars.

In one such shipment, two collector employees of a Flint, Mich., bank found 500 1904-O Morgan dollars, which at the time were cataloging at $375 each. Unfortunately for the would-be-rich bank employees, others were also acquiring examples, and values plummeted. Soon the coins were selling at only $10 each.

The poster child for this type of riches-to-rags scenario, however, is the 1903-O Morgan dollar. It once sold at more than $1,000, but was soon worth a fraction of that.

The 1903-O Morgan was considered very rare.

★★★

Even into the 1960s, when economic historian Paul M. O'Leary again raised the specter of a "crime" in the passage of the Coinage Act of 1873, few argued that there had been this wrongdoing.

Milton Freedman proclaimed in his 1994 book *Money Mischief: Episodes in Monetary History* that no one has ever been able to prove there was even an inkling of misdoing in the passage of this seminal piece of legislation. Much earlier, Neil Carothers wrote in *Fractional Money: A History of Small Coins and Fractional Paper Currency of the United States* that "Not one party to the passage of 1873 recognized the significance of the abolition of the legally existing double standard.... Neither the general public nor Congress realized what this law accomplished. If the silver mining interests had understood what the measure meant they would have aroused in Congress a storm of opposition."

Friedman suffered under the influence of two 20th-century economic historians who overlooked evidence to the contrary (or twisted it to fit a pre-drawn conclusion). In Carothers' case, you only have to look at Mint Director Henry R. Linderman's annual report for 1873 in which Linderman titled the section on the results of the coinage measure: "Gold the Standard or Measure of Value: Silver Subsidiary" to see that at least one major player in the dropping of the silver dollar (the measure's co-author) fully understood what the coinage measure accomplished.

As for the wishful thinking about the silver interests rising up in protest had they realized the silver dollar had been removed from the coinage bill, there's not really much weight to the argument when you realize that the major silver interests at the time, Ralston and his cohorts, supported the elimination of the silver dollar and its replacement with a trade coin for use in the Orient, and that they were paying Linderman to get what they wanted.

Malice of forethought

In "The Scene of the Crime of 1873: A Note," in the August 1960 issue of the *Journal of Political Economy*, Paul M. O'Leary tried to raise the specter of a crime by limiting his focus to Linderman. He argued that there was no reason for the silver-producing interests to be concerned with the Coinage Act of 1873, which they would have viewed merely as a technical revision of the nation's coinage laws and the administration of its assay offices

★★★

and mints. "Under the conditions then prevailing it seems not unreasonable to believe that silver-producing interests could be caught unprepared," O'Leary concluded.

The same, however, was not true, according to O'Leary, of Linderman, an avowed gold standard advocate. Having noticed that Linderman had predicted the coming decline in silver as part of the aforementioned Nov. 19, 1872, report to Treasury Secretary Boutwell (nearly three months prior to the bill's final passage), O'Leary charged that Linderman didn't properly inform Congress of his specialized knowledge of the future market for silver as part of a calculated hostility toward the use of silver in the nation's monetary system.

However, O'Leary failed to note that Linderman's report was anything but hidden, having received contemporary press coverage prior to the bill's passage, or that it served as the impetus behind Boutwell's clear warnings to Congress on Dec. 2, 1872, about the future for silver and his recommendations for a new trade coin. In fact, Boutwell's report was also the subject of press coverage, including from the *New York Times*, which presented its contents in full in its Dec. 3, 1872, issue.

O'Leary also errantly dismissed the introduction of the Trade dollar as an appeasement by Linderman to the silver-producing interests. According to O'Leary, although Linderman was clearly a gold standard advocate, he was not hostile to the silver producers, as evidenced by his suggestions of a trade coin to absorb excess silver.

The 412.5-grain silver dollar could have served the same purpose (shipment to the Orient), O'Leary reasoned, except that, with its full legal-tender status, it could have caused problems in the United States, driving out the gold dollar as silver depreciated. This was something, O'Leary said, Linderman was determined to prevent.

As years of research by numismatic historians and contemporary reports confirm, silver producers on the Pacific coast found little such use for the 412.5-grain silver dollar, as the Chinese would not accept the coin to any degree. Pacific coast merchants and bankers were forced, therefore, to buy the heavier Mexican dollars, at a premium, for use in their trade with this market. This was made clear in a detailed report from David A. Bailey, U.S. Consul

★★★

at Hong Kong, which received considerable press coverage and was brought to the attention of Congress by Boutwell just prior to the mint bill's passage.

O'Leary's charges of a gold standard "malice of forethought" conspiracy have since become largely accepted, at least within economic history circles.

More conspirators

In 1967, Allen Weinstein found that O'Leary was basically correct. Weinstein, however, expanded the cast of characters who secreted their knowledge of the pending downturn in silver from Congress to include Treasury Secretary Boutwell and Sen. John Sherman. Sherman was head of the Senate Finance Committee during the bill's movement through Congress and a popular target for later free silver writers as a conspirator in the supposed "Crime of 1873."

Under Weinstein's version of the "Crime of 1873," first published in the September 1967 issue of the *Journal of American History* below the title "Was There a 'Crime of 1873'?: The Case of the Demonetized Dollar," these three government officials worked to secure passage of the mint bill before monetary inflationists became aware of silver's future availability for their purposes.

LUCKY CALL

Bingo! That might have been the lucky call when, in 1989, an Illinois collector discovered that his bingo change included the fourth 1921-D Morgan dollar released of the first 100 struck at the Denver Mint. It was engraved "4th Dollar Released From 1st 100/Ever Coined At Denver Mint/ Thomas Annear Supt."

Other examples are known with other numbers. However, it is doubtful that all of the first 100 coined were so engraved, as the highest numbered piece currently is 12.

The first Morgan dollar minted by any facility was discovered by researchers Leroy Van Allen and Pete Bishal in 1980 to be in the holdings of the Hayes Museum, part of the Rutherford B. Hayes Presidential Center, Fremont, Ohio.

This specimen is the 10th struck of the first D-mint Morgans.

More recent writers came to accept either O'Leary's or Weinstein's charges. In his 1994 *Money Mischief: Episodes in Monetary History*, Milton Friedman relied heavily on O'Leary's

⭑⭑⭑

analysis in forming the "mischief" portion of his chapter on the "Crime of 1873." However, he left open-ended the question of whether or not such a cover-up rose to the level of a "crime" as defined by the *Oxford English Dictionary.*

According to Friedman, "No allegation of bribery has ever been made, let alone documented, against any individual member of Congress or any government official in connection with the Coinage Act of 1873."

Actually, depending on how you define "bribe" and "government official" in relation to Linderman's actions, this

BLACK GOLD

He was shooting at some food and up from the ground came a bubblin' crude. Oil that is, black gold...Texas tea. He was Jed Clampett on the "Beverly Hillbillies" television show, and in real life actor Buddy Ebsen, who also just happened to be a coin collector.

In 1987 Superior Galleries in Beverly Hills, Calif., was selected by Ebsen to sell his coin collection at auction. Among the coins assembled by Ebsen was a complete type set of U.S. gold coins, a Panama-Pacific Exposition commemorative set in the original copper frame, an 1879 Coiled Hair Stella, and other sets of $2.50, $5 and $20 pieces. He also liked ancients from Greece and Rome.

One of his favorite coins was a nicked-up Territorial $50 gold slug from California. He told *Numismatic News* that: "It's a long way from being Mint State, but I associate a story with each one of these nicks. A story about a family shoving off for the West and this is going to put them in business. And they get attacked by Indians and the coin is stolen and it's in a batch of Wells Fargo coins and highwaymen pick it up or it slides across bars and it pays for prostitutes or all that stuff."

Actor Buddy Ebsen, who played Jed Clampett in "The Beverly Hillbillies."

★★★

was not necessarily true at the time of Friedman's writings —
as a synopsis of the key Linderman-Ralston letters had already
been published in a book outside of the mainstream of economic
research. It certainly was no longer valid with the publication
of the full range of the letters in *Crime of 1873: The Comstock
Connection.*

Though Linderman's use of his influence in Congress as a
former full-time Treasury employee, in return for payment from
the silver interests, may not rise to the level of a bribe (described
in *Webster's* as "money or favor given or promised to a person
in a position of trust to influence his judgment and conduct" or
"something that serves to induce or influence"), it does bring
into question his ethics.

In Linderman's defense, his letters to Ralston show that,
initially, he tried to structure the periods in which he took
payments from the California banker between when he was on
assignment from the Treasury. However, there were serious and
highly visible overlaps when he was functioning as a government
official and when he was working for the bank ring. As one of
the authors of the Coinage Act of 1873, his actions in this regard
continually intermixed.

The Linderman-to-Ralston letters also document that the
major silver-producing interests (i.e., Ralston and his cohorts)
were keenly involved in structuring the contents of the coinage
measure. It is inconceivable, under such a scenario, that they
weren't also aware of the bill's provisions in relation to the gold
standard and the elimination of the standard silver dollar. Both
features were integral parts of the coinage measure throughout
its history, and, contrary to some tellings, were openly discussed
in the House during the bill's movement through Congress.
Contemporary newspaper reports also support this view, as does
a Linderman-to-Ralston letter.

It should be noted also, in this regard, that the same silver
interests who controlled the Comstock during the bill's time before
Congress were not in command of the lode after its passage — a
factor often overlooked by those who contend that, by the late
1870s, Western silver mining interests awoke to the unobserved
removal of their silver dollar, demanding its reinstatement under
the 1878 Bland-Allison Act.

★★★

In March 1873, the first good ore from the Consolidated Virginia mine on the lode began to be hoisted up through the Gould & Curry shaft, and soon, along with the bonanza on the neighboring California, the so-called Bonanza Kings (John W. Mackay, William S. O'Brien, James G. Fair and James C. Flood) came to the forefront on the lode. Ralston and his bank friends were shoved aside.

In 1875, long before the new dollar's introduction, the relationship between Ralston and Linderman ended abruptly. Ralston's speculative ventures had caught up with him. On Aug. 26, 1875, faced with a daylong run by anxious depositors, the effects of which reverberated across the nation, the Bank of California collapsed. The next day, stripped of his livelihood and having forfeited his possessions to the benefit of the bank's creditors, Ralston took his fateful swim in San Francisco Bay.

The Bank of California would reorganize under the leadership of Ralston's Comstock associate, William Sharon, and once again become a leading banking institution.

As for Linderman, he continued to push the gold standard and the Trade dollar up until his death. In 1878, with the passage of the Bland-Allison Act, he directed securing silver for the new coinage. That same year he faced charges of corruption from a congressional investigation into his activities while Mint director.

Among the charges were that he or his wife accepted payments from Pacific coast silver interests for favorable treatment. Linderman vigorously denied all such allegations. However, at least one source claims the strain of doing so led to his death in January 1879.

Considering his previously unknown activities in relation to Ralston (the true "Crime of 1873"), his questionable coin collection, which he assembled while in office and included an 1804 silver dollar, and the incriminating contents of the Linderman-Ralston letters, it's safer to say, in regard to his guilt or innocence in this matter, that such a determination should remain open pending additional research.

★★★

Chapter 15

No More Trades

In 1876 the Trade dollar was demonetized. However, it remained a problem for sometime after.

What's a Trade dollar worth? It depends, of course. In 1883 it was, as a song lyric goes, worth only "85 cents on the dollar." This was because silver had fallen in value and the 420-grain Trade dollar had been demonetized in 1876, three years after its introduction.

The story of the once hated, despised, depreciated U.S. silver dollar known as the Trade dollar is an interesting one. Authorized by the Coinage Act of 1873, the Trade dollar was initially intended for use in trade with the Orient. However, the coinage act allowed the coin a limited legal-tender value in the United States.

★★★

From the moment of its first coining, in mid-1873, the Trade dollar entered domestic circulation. The coins, which could be tendered only in small payments, but could be minted at the request of any silver depositor, quickly became a drug on the market. With the fall of silver, brought on by several factors including the Bonanza strike at Virginia City, Nev.'s, Comstock Lode, Trade dollars depreciated well below their dollar face value.

Those who accepted the coins at face value, often in payment as wages, did so at a significant loss. Soon banks and merchants began refusing to take the coins or offered to do so only at a price near the coin's bullion value.

In 1883, by which time the Trade dollar had been demonetized for seven years, merchants in New York organized a boycott against the unwanted dollar. The boycott even had its own popular song, "respectfully dedicated to the United States Government" — the last verse and chorus for which went:

DOESN'T STACK UP

When the Peace dollar was released, it was quickly attacked, not only for its design, but also because it wouldn't stack properly. Both of these concerns led to rumors that the coins would be recalled by the Mint. A Feb. 2, 1922, press dispatch from New York reported:

Future financiers, now operating as messenger boys in Wall street, have started a drive to corner the newly coined 'Peace' silver dollar, it was learned today. The coins, of which slightly more than a million were minted, are selling at a premium of twenty-five to fifty cents each — the youthful buyers playing a 'hunch' that the issue will be recalled because of criticism of its design and its general make-up, which does not admit of easy stacking.[1]

Mint Director Raymond T. Baker was left to calm fears with an announcement that the coins would not be withdrawn. Baker scolded that "designs for dollars or any other form of currency are not made up to suit the arbitrary whims of the Director." Rather, the designs were submitted to eight leading sculptors and passed by a committee of artists.[2]

* * *

MELTING DOLLARS

In 1918 the Pittman Act brought about the melting of more than 270 million silver dollars. Even with this melting, millions of Morgan dollars had been coined as the result of congressional actions including the Bland-Allison Act of 1878 and the 1890 Sherman Silver Purchase Act.

More than 270 million silver dollars were melted in 1918.

AFRICA BOUND

If it's rare, it must have been lost at sea. The 1799 large cent was not spared such rumors, one of which claimed that the coins sank with a ship bound from Salem, Mass., to the coast of Africa.

The 1799 cent is a rarity, but not because the mintage was lost at sea.

Americans will never be later
Than others to greet all that's fair,
But when we are cheated on all hands,
It's time for a change to appear.
We honor the flag we shall all see
At home, at abroad, or at sea.
But now it has come to a standpoint,
No more trade dollars for me.

With eighty-five cents on the dollar,
Paid out to him night and by day,
What shall we do with this dollar?
Just ask what the Chinamen say.

It took until 1887 before the government agreed to redeem Trade dollars at face value, in exchange for lighter, 412.5-grain silver dollars or subsidiary silver coins. However, by that time many of the coins had fallen into the hands of speculators, and those who earlier had accepted them in good faith had already absorbed their loss.

★

CHOPPED AS GOOD

What's a chopmark? It was a practice, used by Oriental merchants, of adding a stamped insignia to circulating coins as a means of guaranteeing the silver content of coins paid out. Each firm had its own marks and often, after heavy circulation, the host coins would become completely obliterated by chopmarks.

U.S. Trade dollars, produced from 1873-1878 for use in the Orient (also struck from 1879-1885 but just for sale to collectors), are sometimes found with these marks. The marks indicate some of these coins did circulate in the Far East, despite the consensus that the Trade dollar experiment was largely a failure for the United States.

This Trade dollar carries chopmarks.

★★★

Chapter 16

GSA Sales

An advertisement for the GSA dollar sales.

*T*hey were called "The Coins Jesse James Never Got!" And it's true, he didn't get them, but in fairness, neither did Frank James, Cole Younger, Bob Younger, John Younger, Jim Younger or any other bank-, train- or stagecoach-robbing Western outlaw. Why? Because the coins in question were part of the General Services Administration's June 1, 1973, to July 31, 1973, sale of excess silver dollars still in government vaults — most having languished there since their minting in the 19th century.

★★★

Many of the coins in the GSA sales were minted at the Carson City Mint.

SILVER EXCHANGES

On March 23, 1964, Treasury Secretary C. Douglas Dillon halted exchange of silver dollars for Silver Certificates at the Cash Room of the main Treasury in Washington, D.C. At that point, only 2.9 million of the dollars remained in the vaults (most of which were Carson City dollars). "The coins were the historic Carson City minted pieces of the late 1800s, the disposition of which continues to hang in limbo," *Numismatic News* reported. These would later be part of the GSA sales of dollars in the 1970s and 1980.

★ ★ ★

An original Carson City Mint coinage press. It is still in use to strike medals. The old mint now houses the Nevada State Museum.

★★★

The sale was the second in a series of GSA disposals of nearly 3 million silver dollars, largely from the Carson City Mint, that remained in Treasury hands. The first sale, "The Great Silver Sale," was held from Oct. 31, 1972, to Jan. 31, 1973. Others followed in 1974, wrapping up with "The Last of the Carson City Dollars," running from July 1, 1980, to July 31, 1980.

Shown is the Carson City Mint. Next to it is the "Glenbrook" locomotive of the Tahoe Lumber and Fluming Co. The company provided much of the wood used as supports in the Comstock mines.

Bags and bags of mainly Carson City silver dollars await sorting, grading and packaging for the GSA sales.

★★★

The government hoard included some rarities, but what was remarkable was the percentage of certain relatively low-mintage CC dates from 1880-1885 that were included.

For instance, out of an original mintage of 1,136,000 1884-CC Morgan dollars, the GSA holdings included 962,638 coins (or

CONFEDERATE COINS

Most people know the Confederate States of America issued paper money, but few realized it minted coins. That's largely because specimens are rare. It issued a half dollar and a cent. Neither ever went into full production, and the secret of their existence was kept until after the war. In the case of the copper-nickel Confederate cent, its existence wasn't known until late in 1873 when Robert Lovett Jr., a Philadelphia engraver and diesinker, accidentally spent one in a tavern.

It turned out Lovett had been approached by the Confederacy to produce dies for the coin. He combined a depiction of Liberty on the obverse and a wreath on the reverse.

Only a handful of the original coins were made. Restrikes exist from the original dies in various metals. Plus, there are modern reproductions that have no real value.

The Confederacy produced a small number of cents and half dollars.

***

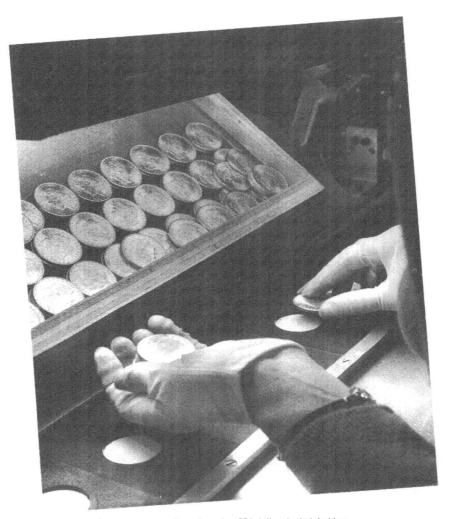

A government employee inserting GSA dollars in their holders.

84.74 percent). The 1885-CC, with a scant mintage of 228,000, would likely otherwise be a rarity. However, 148,285 coins (65.04 percent) survived to be offered by the GSA.

Original mintages and percentages for the other 1880-1885 CC dates not already mentioned included: 1880-CC 591,000 (22.60 percent); 1881-CC 296,000 (49.83 percent); 1882-CC 1,133,000 (53.40 percent); and 1883-CC 1,204,000 (62.75 percent).

★★★

Of the 1884-CC Morgan dollars, 84.74 percent of the original mintage was part of the GSA's offerings.

Although rules for participation varied from sale to sale, "The Coins Jesse James Never Got!" offering was divided into nine sales categories, all of which required participants to place bids. Under GSA rules, a bidder could bid on one coin from each of the nine categories, but no collector could bid on more than nine coins.

If the category sold out, the coins would go to the highest bidders. In one group — "The Potluck!" — the minimum bid was as low as $3 per coin for the offering of 95,000 circulated Morgan and Peace dollars from various mints (You couldn't chose date or mint.) and $5 for the 28,000 uncirculated Morgan and Peace dollars from various mints, also featured in this group.

The highest minimum bid was $30, which applied to several categories of uncirculated CC dollar selections. (A complete breakdown can be found for this and the other sales in *Crime of 1873: The Comstock Connection,* by this author. Krause Publications, 2001).

Jesse James never had any chance to get these coins.

By the conclusion of the Jesse James sale, the GSA had received 1 million bids for 453,000 coins, leaving a little over 1.7 million silver dollars left to be disposed of.

★★★

The 1885-CC Morgan had a relatively low mintage of 228,000. However, 65.04 percent of it was offered in the GSA sales.

The most popular categories were those with the lowest minimum bids. The average bid for circulated coins in the "The Potluck!" was $3.90 per coin, while the average bid for the uncirculated coins was $7.66, but some bids ran up to $200.

Those coins mentioned earlier, with large percentages of their mintages still existing, were the least popular. For instance, of the roughly 521,000 1884-CC dollars offered, just 51,500 bids were received. Minimum bid on these was $30.

Today the GSA sales remain a popular topic among collectors, who can still obtain the coins in original GSA packaging, including those coins Jesse James never got.

★★★

Chapter 17

Roll Craze

It was once popular to collect and speculate in the future value of rolls of U.S. coins.

Coin collecting has known its frenzied periods in which certain coins or rolls of coins are driven up in value, way above what they are reasonably worth. That was the case with the 1950 Jefferson nickel from the Denver Mint. It's still a premium coin, but it's nowhere near as valuable as it once was.

As an article in the Dec. 21, 1959 issue of *Numismatic News* (written during the height of the roll craze) observed, prices for rolls of Jefferson nickels were going through the roof. "There are

★★★

DIME RECALL

Usually it's the general public who first grasps and spreads coinage recall rumors. Not so with the release of the Mercury dime in 1916.

Numismatists in New Orleans advised collectors that placement of designer Adolph Weinman's initials on the coin's obverse violated "the edict which prohibits advertising on the currency of the country," and would soon lead to a recall. Collectors, they said, should save the new coins for "they would likely soon sell at a premium."

Mehl's Numismatic Monthly for January 1917 advised likewise:

> It will be remembered that when the Lincoln penny first was introduced, the designer of that coin was discovered to have labeled the piece with his initials. The treasury did its best to recall the pennies of the type in circulation and new dies were made with the initials eliminated. The same system may be adopted in the case of the new dimes, a press dispatch from Washington says, though $2,850,000 of the new dimes have been coined.[1]

No recall was ever forthcoming. If collectors had looked closely at the reverse of the new Walking Liberty half dollar, also by Weinman, they would have found his initials located on that coin as well, under the tip of the eagle's left wing feathers.

The placement of Adolph Weinman's initials on the Mercury dime led to a rumor that the coins would be recalled.

★★★

The roll craze led to 1950-D Jefferson nickels being driven up to $30 per coin before falling back.

various reasons for this demand," the *News* wrote. "Almost every collector of U.S. coins starts out with the minor denominations. The Jefferson type is a natural collection for the beginner to start with. Most of these coins can be found in circulation with little effort. The next step after completion of a set is usually to improve on the condition of these coins. The ultimate goal is to obtain a brilliant uncirculated set and this is where the scarcity comes in and thus the demand. Also the investors have jumped on the bandwagon and along with the dealers, do brisk business in buying and selling rolls of uncirculated Jeffersons."

The article noted that the average roll price (40 coins) for the 1950-D was $130 (as compared to $5 in 1955), while the 1939-D roll was trading at $1,400 (up from $125 in 1955), the 1939-S was selling for $450 (as compared to $100 in 1955), and the 1942-D was at $400 (up from $42 in 1955). "It must be kept in mind that these prices are the dealers' selling prices for uncirculated rolls," the *News* reported, adding, "One must realize that the high prices on these coins is due in a large degree to the investors and speculators which have entered the field. It is difficult to see how a roll of coins can be included in the collection of a numismatist, either as a thing of beauty or an educational piece."

The 1950-D nickel eventually sold for around $30 before tumbling back.

★★★

Chapter 18

An Indecent Coin

A n age-old hobby story tells that, when Hermon MacNeil's beautiful Standing Liberty quarter was released, the public was outraged. Offended by the blatant display of partial nudity on the coin's figure of Liberty, Americans rose up in protest over the new quarter, causing the Mint to bring coinage to a halt and replace the risqué design with a more demure, fully clothed Liberty.

Is this really the truth behind the creation of this now popular and sought-after coin?

★★★

A vintage hobby tale contends that, when the Standing Liberty quarter was released in 1916, public outcry against the partial nudity on the figure of Liberty led to a halt in coinage early the following year. The design was then changed to feature a chain-mail covering over Liberty's upper torso. However, it was the designer Hermon MacNeil who called for the change, not any public protest, that led to the minting of the Variety 2 coins in 1917.

MacNeil, the artist

It is perhaps ironic that a man who once served as president of the National Sculpture Society — and was awarded medals for his life-size sculptures at expositions in Chicago; Buffalo, N.Y.; Paris; and Charleston, S.C. — should be remembered by numismatists almost exclusively for his design on the Standing Liberty quarter and the controversy supposedly surrounding the Variety 1 coins depicting Liberty with her right breast exposed.

MacNeil, born near Chelsea, Mass., on Feb. 27, 1866, to John Clinton MacNeil and Mary (Lash) MacNeil, was the product of a new age in American sculpture. It was an age in which sculpture gained equal status with other forms of art and was considered by many to be on par with architecture.

He participated in a fruitful era of great expositions that allowed young sculptors — including Augustus Saint-Gaudens, Adolph Weinman, James Earle Fraser, John Flanagan and Victor D. Brenner — a rich creative forum for their artistic endeavors.

Great fairs such as the World's Columbian Exposition in 1893, the Paris Exposition in 1900, the Pan-American Exposition

* ★ *

in 1901, the Louisiana Purchase Exposition in 1904 and the Panama-Pacific Exposition in 1915 were eagerly sought out by artists looking to showcase their talents to the world.

As a youngster, MacNeil attended public schools in Chelsea, where his artistic talents began to blossom and were encouraged. At the urging of his cousin, Jeanette Mitchell, MacNeil entered Massachusetts State Normal Art School. He completed the four-year course, graduating in 1886 with highest honors.

HAMMER AND SICKLE

When Mint engraver Gilroy Roberts affixed his "GR" initials to the Kennedy half dollar, stories circulated that it was the work of a runaway Communist bent on showing his country's hammer and sickle on a U.S. coin.

For the next three years he taught industrial arts at Sibley College — the former name for Cornell University's School of Engineering.

In 1888, at the urging of Sibley's dean, Robert H. Thurston, who recognized MacNeil's artistic and modeling abilities, MacNeil borrowed $500 from his uncle and went to Paris, where he pursued his career in sculpture.

Paris, at the time of MacNeil's arrival, was considered the artistic center for sculptors. American sculptors flocked there to study in the ateliers of French sculptors.

MacNeil studied for three years at the Academie Julian, under the tutelage of Henry Chapu, and at the Ecole des Beaux-Arts, where his teacher was the renowned Jean Falguire. MacNeil absorbed much of the impressionistic modeling of the French school, and its influence remained evident throughout his career.

In 1891 he returned to New York, where he obtained a letter of introduction from Saint-Gaudens to Philip Martiny. Martiny was involved in preparing the sculptural decorations for the World's Columbian Exposition being held in Chicago. MacNeil worked with Martiny and also created two figures of his own design for the Electricity Building at the exposition.

Following the exposition, MacNeil remained in Chicago, where he secured a position teaching modeling during the evenings at the school of the Chicago Art Institute. During the day, he worked on various sculptural projects, including four bas-reliefs

★★★

of Pere Marquette for the Marquette Building in Chicago. The scenes depict the Jesuit priest's life among the Indians in the early days of the settlement of Chicago.

ENTRY WOUND

If it weren't bad enough that Gilroy Roberts' initials on the Kennedy half dollar were touted as Russia's hammer and sickle, others morbidly proclaimed that the location of the initials — at the truncation of the bust of Kennedy — marked the point at which one of Lee Harvey Oswald's bullets struck the president.

Placement of Gilroy Roberts' initials on the Kennedy half dollar led to a bizarre rumor.

MacNeil was fascinated by the American Indian — a theme that would occupy the majority of his sculptural efforts for the next decade. He studied their lifestyles, customs and ceremonies.

In 1895 he took an extensive trip to America's Southwest, traveling through Colorado, Arizona and New Mexico, where he studied the Moquis and Zunis tribes, and was inspired to create several statues.

At summer's end, MacNeil was invited to submit photographs of his works in competition for the Rinehart Scholarship to study in Rome. He won the award and, before leaving for Rome, married one of his students, Carol L. Brooks, a sculptor, who is best remembered artistically for her work *Foolish Virgin.*

The scholarship was originally to last only one year, but it was extended. MacNeil and his wife spent from 1896 to 1900 in Rome.

To meet the scholarship requirements, MacNeil had to create several sculptures. Notable among his works were the bust *Agnese Mattelia* and the sculptures *A Primitive Chant* (modeled after Black Pipe, a destitute Indian he had met in Chicago), *From Chaos Came Light* and *Sun Vow.*

Sun Vow, an enlargement of a sketch he made in Chicago, was apparently inspired by the Sioux Indian Nation's initiation

★★★

Hermon MacNeil was apparently inspired by the Sioux Indian Nation's initiation ceremony in sculpting *Sun Vow.*

ceremony. It depicts an Indian sitting at the side of his adolescent son, who has just shot an arrow toward the sun.

Another work, *Moqui Runner,* is a bronze statuette of an Indian dashing across the desert with a tangle of serpents in his hands — reminiscent of a Prayer for Rain ceremony, which MacNeil had occasion to observe on his trip to America's Southwest.

★★★

In 1899 MacNeil closed his studio at the Villa dell' Aurora and went to Paris for a year, where he worked on the decorations for the U.S. building at the Paris Exposition.

At the Paris Exposition, *Sun Vow* and *Moqui Runner* brought critical acclaim.

Sun Vow won a silver medal in Paris and a year later earned its creator a gold medal at the Pan-American Exposition in Buffalo. It was also exhibited at the Louisiana Purchase Exposition in St. Louis in 1904.

Sun Vow was held in such high esteem that Lorado Taft, in his 1930 *History of American Sculpture,* said, "This group is good enough and important enough to assure its author a permanent place in the history of American art."

Noted sculptor Larado Taft termed Hermon MacNeil's grouping in *Sun Vow* as being good enough to earn MacNeil "...a permanent place in the history of American art."

Photo Courtesy of Positibl.

By the time he returned to New York to establish a studio, MacNeil was already a respected sculptor. Just prior to his return, a special showing of several of his pieces was held in 1899 at New York's esteemed Metropolitan Museum of Art.

After his return, he was asked to do the pedimental decoration for the Anthropological Building at the Pan-American Exposition and a sculptural group, *Despotic Age,* which stood in front of the U.S. government building. His work *Agnese Mattelia,* created in Rome, and another work, *Beatrice,* were also displayed.

MacNeil was also commissioned to design the exposition's official gold award medal. The medal depicts a youthful woman standing beside a buffalo — representing the triumph of intellect over physical power. On the reverse, a North American Indian offers a peace pipe to a South American Indian.

MacNeil also created sculptural pieces for an exposition in Charleston, S.C. An exhibit at the Pratt Institute in Brooklyn, N.Y., had 22 of MacNeil's works, 17 of which were Indian subjects.

For the Louisiana Purchase Exposition in 1904, his sculptural work included an Indian boy running beside a buffalo. For Portland, Ore., he modeled *The Coming of the White Man.*

★★★

In Portland, Ore., MacNeil's *Coming of the White Man* shows an Indian chief (right) and his medicine man.

★ ★ ★

Hermon MacNeil's *McKinley Memorial* in Columbus, Ohio. Below is a scene of the dedication ceremony on Sept. 14, 1906.

Hermon MacNeil was the product of an era in which artists were encouraged to display their creations at major world expositions, including the 1893 World's Columbian Exposition in Chicago.

In 1910 his sculptural work devoted to the Indian was just about ended. For the Panama-Pacific Exposition in 1915, he modeled signs of the zodiac in stylized forms related to abstract art.

Other notable works by MacNeil include the *McKinley Memorial* in Columbus, Ohio; a statue of Ezra Cornell on the campus of Cornell University in Ithaca, N.Y; the *Judge Burke Memorial* in Seattle; a portrait of Judge Ellsworth in Hartford, Conn.; and a bronze figure of Gen. George Rogers Clark in Vincennes, Ind.

★★★

When his quarter dollar was released, Hermon MacNeil was upset with the adopted design on the obverse and the reverse. Of the reverse, he complained that the eagle had been dropped too low (Variety 1 image shown here at bottom). For the revised version (Variety 2), the eagle was moved up and three stars were placed below it.

He created a statue of George Washington for the Washington Arch in New York City; a Pilgrim fathers-and-mothers group in Waterbury, Conn.; a statue of Marquette for Chicago's West Park; a soldiers-and-sailors monument in Albany, N.Y.; *Defenders of Fort Sumter* in Charleston, S.C.; a marble pedimental group for the Supreme Court Building in Washington, D.C.; and a 130-foot-long bas-relief frieze for the Missouri State Capitol.

★★★

A small but important work

It is, therefore, readily apparent that in terms of physical size, MacNeil's much-acclaimed Standing Liberty quarter was the smallest of his works. In relation to numismatics and its place in U.S. coinage history, it is, however, one of his most important and the most beautiful. Three letters obtained by coin dealer Michael C. Annis in 1987 formed the basis of an article by this writer in a 1988 issue of *Coins* magazine, which explored the background of the artist and re-examined the story behind the quarter's release, leading to the conclusion that the design change in 1917 was not due to public protest over nudity on the Type I quarter.[1]

The letters in question came from the estate of Cecilia W. (Muench) MacNeil, whom MacNeil married in 1946, following the death of his first wife, two years prior.

The first letter, dated Oct. 26, 1900, is a handwritten introduction from Henry Mitchell, a gem and seal engraver from Boston, to a Mr. Tiffe in Buffalo.

The letter introduces Mitchell's nephew, MacNeil, "of whom I spoke when I had the pleasure of calling upon you at Marlboro." It continues, "He [MacNeil] has just written me that he was about to go to your City on business connected with the Exposition."

This letter was apparently written in connection with the Pan-

> **DISARMING BELIEF**
>
> The Peace dollar, minted from 1921-1935, was a prime target for criticism and misconception. Its story is well documented in the pages of *The Numismatist*, as are the outcries from the general press captured in February and March 1922 issues of the American Numismatic Association's journal.
>
> News that the early designs for the new coin included one showing a broken sword led to the mistaken belief that the coin had been inspired by the Conference on the Limitation of Armaments being held at that time in Washington, D.C.
>
> The *New York Herald*, for example, said that, although a new silver dollar symbolic of an era of peace was a good idea, in attempting to portray the idea behind the disarmaments conference, the artist showed an eagle standing on a broken sword — the symbol either of surrender, a battle lost, or that the sword's owner had disgraced himself.
>
> "But America has not broken its sword," the *Herald* challenged. "It has not been cashiered or beaten; it has not lost allegiance to itself. The blade is bright and keen and wholly dependable."[1]

★★★

FAST RUNNING COWARD

Eagles have been under assault for a number of years, not only in nature, but also in the nature of how they are portrayed on U.S. coins. Just about every time a new coin has been issued, someone has complained about its eagle. From the scrawny eagle found on the 1792 half dismes and 1794 dollars to modern U.S. coinage, the cry of foul has arisen.

Some of the complaints have been totally erroneous, others just plain silly. Take, for example, a 1925 press dispatch from New York in which Harmon Pumpelly Read of Albany criticized the eagle on the new Standing Liberty quarter.

Using a 1904 Barber quarter and a 1920 Standing Liberty quarter as props, he argued that the new eagle broke the rules of heraldry. Read said:

> On the old coin the eagle is in an upright position with wings extended, conveying the symbol of power and empire. The eagle is facing forward — that is bravery. The eagle on the new coin is not an American eagle. It is facing in the wrong direction. No power and emphasis here. That bird signifies cowardice. The fact that it is winging across the coin symbolizes speed, I suppose. A coward, and a fast running one.[2]

One critic thought the eagle on the Standing Liberty quarter looked like a coward.

American Exposition and may have, in some way, been tied to MacNeil's work on the medal for that exposition.

Mitchell is, in all likelihood, the uncle who generously loaned the young sculptor the $500 he needed to pursue his studies in Paris. Mitchell's daughter, Jeanette Mitchell, as has been previously observed, is said to have encouraged the young artist to attend the Massachusetts State Normal Art School.

The letter was written on Mitchell's personalized stationery, which advised, "Medal Dies Engraved and Medals Struck in Gold, Silver and Bronze."

Mitchell, the son of sculptor F.N. Mitchell, was a prominent medalist of the period. His medallic works are strewn throughout R.W. Julian's *Medals of the United States Mint: The First Century 1792-1892*. One of Mitchell's most important works was an award medal for the U.S. Centennial in 1876.

Mitchell was so highly regarded that, according to Q. David Bowers in *The History of United States Coinage: As Illustrated by the Garrett Collection*, when the Treasury Department

★★★

The Treasury Department's official notification to Hermon MacNeil of the acceptance of his designs for the quarter dollar.

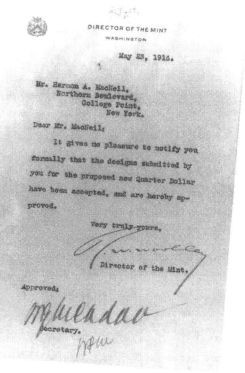

Treasury Secretary William G. MacAdoo.

proposed design changes in 1890, Mitchell was included among possible design-competition judges, along with Saint-Gaudens and Charles Barber.

A letter of introduction from Mitchell must have, therefore, carried considerable weight, and one can readily assume MacNeil put it to good use.

The second letter held by Annis, and the most significant in relation to the Standing Liberty quarter design, was a notification of the Treasury Department's acceptance of MacNeil's design.

Dated May 23, 1916, this typewritten letter, on the Mint director's official stationery, was signed by Mint Director R.W. Woolley and Treasury Secretary William G. McAdoo. It read, "It gives me great pleasure to notify you formally that the designs submitted by you for the proposed new Quarter Dollar have been accepted, and are hereby approved."

An unsigned copy of this letter (but on stationery headed by the words "Treasury Department") appears in J.H. Cline's

★★★

Standing Liberty Quarters. Cline also reproduced several other important letters that help to piece together the history of MacNeil's quarter.

In 1915 MacNeil was selected, along with Weinman and one other artist from a field of 50 entrants, to submit designs for the redesign of the nation's subsidiary silver coinage.

MacNeil was notified of his selection — along with Weinman and an artist named Polasek — by a letter from Woolley dated Dec. 28, 1915.

In the event that one of his designs was accepted, MacNeil would be paid $2,000. If, however, his designs were rejected, he would be compensated the meager sum of $300.[2]

MacNeil expressed displeasure over the proposed $300 compensation in a letter to Woolley on Jan. 4, 1916. In this same letter, he asked for a clarification of the department's April 15 deadline for design submission and the design requirements in regard to his treatment of the representation of Liberty.[3]

MacNeil also acknowledged that he had visited the Mint during the previous week, where he discussed coinage requirements with Mint engraver Barber and George Morgan.

MacNeil officially accepted the Treasury's commission in a letter dated Jan. 11, 1916.

In a subsequent letter, he told Woolley that the three sculptors had agreed to have preliminary designs ready for submission by mid-February. He said he expected all three artists would submit their material to arrive in Washington on Feb. 21.

Mint Engraver George Morgan.

This timetable must have been adhered to, because on Feb. 28 Woolley notified MacNeil (informally) that the Treasury Department had accepted one of

★★★

MacNeil's models for the quarter's obverse. In other words, the letter explained, MacNeil had been awarded "one-half design out of a possible three designs."[4]

The official notification came on May 23, 1916. Two weeks prior to the official notification, Woolley wrote to MacNeil, in the third letter owned by Annis, "I thank you for your note of recent date, and beg you to say I shall be in New York on Wednesday, when I would like to talk to you about data for a description of the coin."

Apparently, even though formal notification had not yet been sent to the artist, the department was already working on the official written description of the design elements on MacNeil's quarter.

This was, perhaps, for inclusion in the Mint director's report of July 15, 1916, which was the first official description of the design.

Woolley wrote the following of the quarter:

> The design of the 25-cent piece is intended to typify in a measure the awakening interest of the country to its own protection.... In the new design Liberty is shown as a full-length figure, front view, with head turned toward the left, stepping forward to the gateway of the country, and on the wall are inscribed the words 'In God We Trust,' which words also appear on the new half dollar, mentioned above. The left arm of the figure of Liberty is upraised, bearing the shield in the attitude of protection, from which the covering is being drawn. The right hand bears the olive branch of peace. On the field above the head is inscribed the word 'Liberty,' and on the step under her feet '1916.' The reverse of this coin necessitates by law a representation of the American eagle, and is here shown in full flight, with wings extended, sweeping across the coin.[5]

Lead impressions from the die for the quarter were submitted to Mint Director F.J.H. von Engelken by Superintendent A.M. Joyce on Oct. 13, 1916, with silver impressions following shortly thereafter.

★★★

MacNeil complains

On Jan. 11, 1917, shortly after the coins entered circulation, MacNeil wrote to Von Engelken complaining that the coins as issued had "a resemblance to" a design he made the prior spring, one that he later "changed and modified considerably" with approval of the Mint director and the Treasury secretary. He was therefore surprised to see this discarded early modeling on the quarter in circulation.[6]

SHY MODEL

Up until the early 1970s, numismatists were pretty well in agreement that Doris Doscher, a model from Whitson, N.Y., had posed for Hermon MacNeil's Standing Liberty quarter, released in 1916. As early as 1917 *The Numismatist* had reported the same.

In 1972, however, Irene MacDowell, then 92, came forward as having posed for MacNeil. MacDowell was the wife of Hermon MacNeil's tennis partner and a close family friend. MacDowell claimed to have posed for the design for a period of 10 days before her husband objected. A decision, it is said, was made among all parties involved to keep her service as a model a secret.[3]

It is chronologically important to remember that, even though 52,000 1916-dated coins were minted, none of these coins reached circulation until late 1916 or early 1917.

Although the Mint had hoped to have the new coins in circulation by July 1916, it ran into problems with production of the new dies, causing it to delay issue and work nights striking coins of the old design in order to meet the demands of commerce.[7]

The January 1917 issue of *The Numismatist*, likely sent to subscribers in December 1916, reports on the design for the new quarter, but admits that at press time none of the new subsidiary coins had been placed into circulation. An article by Henry Hettger and Susan Novac in the July/August 1994 issue of Bowers and Merena's *Rare Coin Review* quotes the Jan. 17, 1917, issue of the Philadelphia *Public Ledger* as recording that "the new silver quarter is at hand and in circulation."

It is, therefore, likely MacNeil's Jan. 11, 1917, letter of complaint to Von Engelken represents the artist's first glimpse of the finished product — the 1916 Type I quarter bearing a design similar to one he discarded the prior spring.

MacNeil said that after receiving the coins, he went directly to the Mint, where he "was still more surprised and interested

★★★

The Variety 2 Standing Liberty quarter appeared in 1917.

to see the many variations that had already been on this coin, many of them arrangements that I myself had already tried and discarded."[8]

He told Von Engelken that, in the interest of producing the best possible design, certain modifications were needed.

For the obverse, MacNeil suggested moving Liberty's head away from the rim, preventing the figure from becoming bowlegged, and minimizing the sagging of the shield by having it pulled tighter.

For the reverse, MacNeil said the eagle had been dropped too low, which made it look (when soiled) as if the tail was connected with the lettering below. He said this gave the appearance of a low-flying or just-rising eagle, and that from his study of the bird, the talons are only extended behind when the eagle is well under way at high altitude.

He suggested that the Mint may have lowered the eagle to prevent its right wing from touching the "A" in "America" — a feature he liked and one that would reappear on the modified 1917 design.[9]

The text of Von Engelken's Jan. 13 reply can be found in Don Taxay's *The U.S. Mint and Coinage: An Illustrated History From 1776 to the Present.* The director informed MacNeil that "as the coins have gone into circulation, no marked changes could be undertaken."[10]

Von Engelken cautioned that "no radical changes would be considered," and that he reserved the right not to have new dies

★★★

made, should the new model depart from the accepted design.

Changes were made, however, incorporating not only the features called for in MacNeil's Jan. 11 letter, but to the figure of Liberty, as well.

A reason for the change

In a notice datelined from Washington Feb. 6, 1917, it was announced that the Mint was considering slight changes to the design at MacNeil's request, noting that:

> Treasury officials are considering the matter on the suggestion of the designer of the coins Herman McNeill [sic] of New York. McNeill [sic] is said to have suggested placing on the obverse [sic, reverse] side of the coin a background of stars against the figure of the eagle and slightly raising the design of the eagle.[11]

In an April 16, 1917, letter to Rep. William Ashbrook, chairman of the House Committee on Coinage, Weights, and Measures, McAdoo said similarly (in reference to an act to modify the design) that the modifications proposed were considered "slight."

The changes included, according to McAdoo, the raising of the eagle on the reverse, the addition of three stars beneath the eagle, rearrangement of the lettering, and the addition of a slight concavity to the surface.

McAdoo concluded, "I am sorry to have to ask for this change, but since the original dies were made the artist has found that they are not true to the original design and that a great improvement can be made in the artistic value and appearance of the coin by making the slight changes the act contemplates."[12]

The act (H.R. 3548), approved July 9, 1917, is reprinted in the Mint director's report for 1917 and confirms that the changes were of an artistic nature and were to be in place by July 1, 1918.

MacNeil apparently found all of the changes acceptable. In an Aug. 13, 1917, letter, he wrote to Mint Director R.S. Baber, "I am much pleased to get your announcement that the Quarter Dollar is lawfully back to an artistic basis and is now being minted."[13]

★★★

As an interesting side note to MacNeil's concern over the Mint's alterations to his design (as it appeared on the 1916 and 1917 Type I coins), in 1988 Bowers and Merena Inc. of Wolfeboro, N.H., auctioned a presentation frame containing a 1916 Standing Liberty quarter and a handwritten letter from MacNeil written on the same date (Jan. 11, 1917) as his letter of complaint to Von Engelken about the Mint's substitution of designs.

The frame was included in Bowers and Merena's sale of the Lloyd M. Higgins, M.D., Collection, held Jan. 28-30, 1988, in Los Angeles.

The letter, presented with the quarter, is addressed to a Walter M. Pratt of Boston. It states:

WRONG 'O'

When the Franklin half dollar was released in 1948, rumors sprang up, as they had with the dime, that Sinnock's initials on the half dollar represented Joseph Stalin. The coin's reverse also created a stir when it was rumored that the placement of a small "o" in the word "of" in "United States of America", had been a mistake, and the coins would be recalled. The same story circulated for the Memorial reverse of the Lincoln cent upon its release in 1959.

A small "o" in "of" on the back of the Franklin half dollar brought out recall rumors.

> If per adventure you should be tempted to make any publicity of the little quarter — it might be well to wait a bit as they are not issued yet & I am making a stand for improvements. As I told you they have garbled my design.[14]

Protest lacking

The March 1917 issue of *The Numismatist* gave the first inkling of a redesign, saying that press dispatches from Washington contained information that change was being contemplated. MacNeil, it said, had suggested placing a background of stars around the eagle and slightly raising its design.[15]

The primary design changes were made to the reverse, said Farran Zerbe, with the eagle placed higher, and a new arrangement

★★★

of stars. Of the obverse, he said, "the features of the head of Liberty are stronger. The sprig in her hand does not engage the 'L.' There are fewer dots in the shield, and the undraped chaste bust of the old has been given what looks like a corsage of mail."[16]

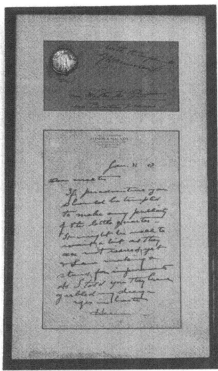

Written on Jan. 11, 1917, the same day MacNeil complained to the Treasury Department about the design of the quarter, this letter confirms that MacNeil planned on "making a stand for improvements."

Under the heading "Miss Liberty Now in a Gown of Mail?" the editorial in the same issue of *The Numismatist* did question the intention of the designer in placing Liberty in the new covering, wondering if it had anything to do with the country's movement from a state of "preparedness" displayed on the initial design to one reflecting its subsequent entry into World War I.[17]

Beyond artistic considerations, the only other concern raised in House and Senate debate over the design change was the coin's inability to properly stack, a concern addressed in the redesign and likely of importance in the decision to grant the artist his concessions.

Following the alterations, MacNeil's Standing Liberty quarter continued to be minted through 1930, with one other design change in 1925. At that time, the date was lowered to protect it from wear.

MacNeil died in October 1947, more than 30 years after his quarter first entered circulation.

With his passing he left a legacy of great American sculpture, including one of the finest coins ever produced.

★★★

Chapter 19

Small and Large Dates

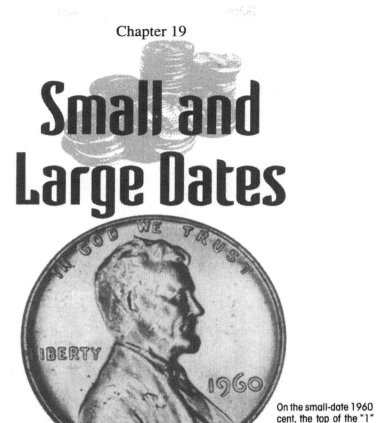

On the small-date 1960 cent, the top of the "1" aligns with the top of the "9."

Several minor varieties in the cent series have sparked interest in pocket change over the years and some can still be found in circulation, the small and large dates of 1960, 1970 and 1982, for example.

In 1960 a change in the master dies led to so-called small- and large-date cents being minted at Philadelphia and Denver. The small-date variety is more valuable and can be distinguished from its large-date counterpart by the more compact appearance of the "6" and its shorter tail. Another diagnostic is that the top of the "1" on the small-date cent aligns with the top of the "9." On the large-date, the numerals are also slightly closer together.

★★★

For the 1970-S small date (the more valuable), the top part of the loop of the "9" is a key. On the large-date specimen, it curves at a 45-degree angle toward the leg of the "9."

On the small-date coin, the loop turns more sharply toward the body of the "9." The position of the "7" in the date is also important. On the large-date cent, the "7" appears to rest just below the remaining three digits in the date. On the small-date coin, the top of all four digits are in line. A comparison in the April 14, 1979, issue of *Numismatic News* found that the large-date specimens had more rounded rims and the small-date coins had thicker and squarer rims.

1982 was a big year for the cent, which changed from a brass composition to copper-coated zinc. It was also the year of more large- and small-date cents. These can be found on brass 1982 coins as well as the new copper-coated zinc coins. Circulation coinage at West Point, Denver and proofs were of the large-date variety. Philadelphia began coinage with the large-date dies before switching to the small-date dies in September 1982. The small-date die featured letters and date with strongly beveled edges and a slightly lower relief to Lincoln's bust. The "8" in the date was also repositioned and on the small-date variety appears more in line with the other numerals. The upper loop of the "8" is also noticeably smaller than the lower loop.

MISSING MINTMARKS

OK. So in the 19th century not many coin collectors even noticed that some coins, those produced at branch mints, carried letters (mintmarks) denoting where the coins were struck, or that some of the mintmarked coins were scarcer than those struck in Philadelphia. By the 20th century, however, collecting was not only by date, but also by date and mintmark. Thus, it's not hard to imagine the outrage experienced by collectors when, faced with a coinage shortage, the U.S. Mint stopped putting mintmarks on U.S. coins in 1965.

Why had the marks been stopped? Because the Treasury had come to the ill-founded belief that the coin shortage was being caused by collectors, and if it removed the mintmarks, coins would remain in circulation. By 1968 the lunacy had lifted and the mintmarks were restored to these common coins.

Fear of hoarding by collectors led to this half dollar being minted without a mintmark.

★★★

MISSING 'P'

There have been instances when mintmarks have been inadvertently left off of proof coins minted for collectors, creating instant rarities, including the 1968, 1970, 1975, and 1983 dimes. In 1982 it wasn't a proof issue that sent collectors scrambling, but a circulation dime that lacked a mintmark. By that year, Philadelphia had been placing its "P" mintmark on coins above the cent, and the dime should have carried either a P or a D (for Denver). It wasn't long before reports filled hobby newspapers about the finds of "no mintmark" 1982 Roosevelt dimes from the Philadelphia Mint, which were turning up in small hoards.

GENTLY WEEPING

What guitar starts out with six strings on the headstock and tapers to five strings along the neck and body? It's the one depicted on the 2002 Tennessee quarter. Sharp-eyed collectors quickly noticed the discrepancy, which was explained away by the U.S. Mint as artistic license and the problems with working with a small, three-dimensional design.

"Artistic license" was claimed as a defense of the 2002 Tennessee state quarter.

WITHDRAWAL WOES

When the announcement came that the San Francisco Mint was closing its doors in 1955, the rumor mills were ripe. Half dollars, dimes, and cents, the only coins struck for circulation that year bearing the "S" mintmark, were hoarded in the wake of tales of a recall.

★

Chapter 20

Seeing Double

The 1955 doubled-die cents are easy to spot.

Some people probably thought they were seeing double or that their vision was blurred when they first saw a 1955 doubled-die Lincoln cent. It was one of the most recognizable doublings on a U.S. coin. The date is widely doubled, as are the legends, including the motto "In God We Trust."

It was created (as was a 1972 doubled-die cent) when working dies (those that struck the planchets to produce the coins) were mistakenly doubled in the process of the transfer of the designs from the working hubs. All subsequent coins struck from such dies would show the doubling. However, as dies are replaced after a period of use, the number of doubled coins to reach

★★★

The popular and widely doubled 1972 doubled-die cent caused a stir when it began to turn up in circulation.

WATCHFUL WAITING

Designer Adolph Weinman's initials, "AW," on the Mercury dime's obverse, which were mistaken by some to be a single "W," set people to wondering if the initial stood for then-President Woodrow Wilson. Or, with the escalating concerns of war in Europe, "watchful waiting."[1]

MULE DOLLARS

It had the right reverse, but the wrong obverse. In 2000, collectors were surprised by the existence of a small number of coins with the quarter dollar obverse design and the reverse design from Sacagawea dollar. Termed a "mule," the error coin was struck on a golden dollar planchet.

collectors was limited, making the 1955 doubled-die cent a high-priced oddity. The 1972 doubled die is no slouch, either.

Frankly, for those interested in error coins (which used to be known to collectors as "freaks") there are any number of them, from the common to the ultra rare, that can be collected and sometimes still show up in change, including a 1983 Lincoln cent with a doubled ear and a 1943 Jefferson nickel with a doubled eye.

In the 1800s dates were often changed on coinage dies to save on die steel, leading to some spectacular and rare overdates like the 1825/4 half eagle. In the 20th century you find such classics as the 1918/7-D Buffalo nickel, the 1942/1 and 1942/1-D Mercury dimes, the 1918/7-S Standing Liberty quarter and various desirable overmintmarks.

★ ★ ★

Chapter 21

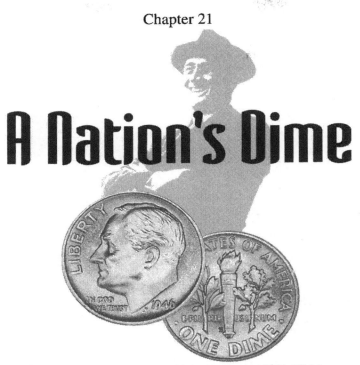

A Nation's Dime

The Roosevelt dime was released into circulation in 1946. Official announcement of its release was made from the White House on Jan. 30 by President Harry S. Truman and Franklin D. Roosevelt Jr.

*D*id John R. Sinnock design the Roosevelt dime or did Dr. Selma H. Burke? At first glance this might seem like an easy question to answer.

Tradition holds that former Mint chief engraver John R. Sinnock designed the coin now used by millions of Americans. His initials appear on it, and all credit has gone to him in the past and likely will continue to do so in the future. But is this right? Or is it possible that Burke, who died in 1995 at the age of 94, was correct in her unending belief that Sinnock plagiarized her design from a life-study she did of President Franklin D. Roosevelt in the early 1940s, giving her no credit whatsoever?

★★★

Selma Burke with an unidentified bust. An accomplished sculptor, Burke founded the Selma Burke School of Sculpture and the Selma Burke Art Center.

Photograph by Robert R. Van Ryzin.

Selma Burke, as she appeared in 1993 at the age of 94.

★ ★ ★

Marked success

Frankly, the passage of time has made discovering what is the truth in the question of Burke's claim virtually impossible. Many of the principals and potential witnesses to what may have been an injustice against one of the nation's leading sculptors have passed on.

Also, given the fact that Burke was black, many have discounted any claim she may have to the design purely on the basis of her skin color. This is a shame and an injustice of its own, but it's how this story has been viewed by some.

Yet even those who elect to dismiss Burke's claim, either upon a simplistic judgment made on the basis of race or because of absence of definitive proof, would have to admit that in Burke there is a story of marked success — a story of a woman who went up against remarkable odds to come out on top. It is an interesting story in its own right and worthy of retelling.

There is the delightful personal account of a lady who met with the president, charmed him, modeled him from life and used this work as a stepping stone to a career matched by few and replete with major awards and accomplishments. Also, there is the story of a genuinely warm, charming person who honestly, and deeply, believed she had been wronged and wanted to set the record straight.

Perhaps, above all, there is the story of the coin and the need to re-examine what we know and don't know of its creation — if

SEEING RED

Tales of subversive acts by foreign powers and attempts to impress their ideologies on Americans are certainly not new in this country. It's probably not that surprising then that those who revel in defending the United States against unseen enemies would scrutinize U.S. coins for evidence of foreign intrigue.

One of the best-known rumors about Communists infiltrating the U.S. Mint is that the initials "JS" on the Roosevelt dime, issued in 1946, stood for Joseph Stalin. So pervasive was this story that Mint Director Nellie Tayloe Ross found it necessary to publicly refute the claim, explaining that the initials belonged to Mint engraver John Sinnock.

Certain ambitious versions of this bit of nonsense add that President Franklin D. Roosevelt had promised to place Stalin's initials on the coin when he met with the Communist ruler at the Yalta Conference in February 1945. This assuming that Roosevelt knew his portrait would appear on the dime after his death. He didn't.

★★★

Courtesy of August Swain.

Burke's bronze *Mother and Child*.

for no other reason than to offer the numismatic community additional food for thought and to bring home the point that history is not chiseled in stone. There's often room for legitimate speculation when it comes to what is regarded as fact.

How Burke entered the picture and how she came to the solid conviction that credit for designing the Roosevelt dime belonged to her was explored by this writer in an extensive interview with Burke in July 1993 at her studio in Pennsylvania.

Faithful portrayal

To fully tell the story we must, however, begin at an earlier point, following Roosevelt's death on April 12, 1945, when efforts began to honor him on a coin. The idea was to have the coin designed, engraved, and ready to place into circulation in conjunction with the March of Dimes campaign the following year. The president, it was thought, had been afflicted by polio and proceeds from the March of Dimes campaign would go to fight the disease.

★★★

Work on the new dime design, which would replace Adolph Weinman's Winged Liberty or Mercury motif (minted since 1916), began immediately. On Oct. 12, 1945, Sinnock submitted models to Acting Mint Director Leland Howard, who sent the models to the Commission of Fine Arts.

Photos of these early models, and additional details of the commission's reaction to Sinnock's design, can be found in Don Taxay's *U.S. Mint and Coinage: An Illustrated History From 1776 to the Present.*

Taxay quotes commission chairman Gilmore Clarke, who complained in an Oct. 22, 1945, letter to Howard that the modeling of Roosevelt's head was not good and

Burke said that, when she entered the competition to design the plaque for the new Recorder of Deeds building in Washington, D.C., she found it difficult to find profiles of the president. Most photographs showed him three-quarters face and smiling.

needed more dignity. Clarke wrote, "It may be that the position of the head — the angle at which it is placed on the background — and the shape and ending of the neck are at fault."[1]

The commission also made suggestions for changes to the reverse design and preferred a modeling of a torch with branches on each side rather than another showing a hand holding a torch.

Sinnock reworked the models for the obverse, which were again submitted and again rejected. The commission suggested a competition be held among five prominent artists (Edward McCartan, James Earle Fraser, Paul Manship, Adolph A. Weinman and Jo Davidson) to obtain a better design. This was rejected, however, because of the short time frame set for introduction of the new coin.[2]

Official announcement of the new coin was made from the White House by President Harry S. Truman and Franklin D. Roosevelt Jr. on Jan. 30, 1946 — what would have been the late president's 64th birthday.

★★★

Eleanor Roosevelt complained to Burke the image of her husband by Burke made him look too young.

The new dime was readily accepted by the public and generally praised. Its adoption was another step in a conversion from allegorical designs; only the half dollar remained.

Writing of the dime's design, Cornelius Vermeule, in his *Numismatic Art in America: Aesthetics of the United States Coinage,* was effusive over its portrayal of Roosevelt. Vermeule wrote, "He [Sinnock] demonstrated his long practice and superior craftsmanship as a die-designer in producing a clean, satisfying, and modestly stylish, no-nonsense coin that in total view comes forth with notes of grandeur."[3]

Vermeule then compared Sinnock's work to that of 18th-century French sculptor Jeane Antoine Houdon, who had sculpted a famed bust of Washington from life.

"Houdon never modeled Roosevelt in clay and plaster nor carved him in marble, but had he done so the results would have surely resembled the profile on the dime," Vermeule said. "The die-designer has achieved a precise, detailed portrait which shows full force of character amid a faithful portrayal."[4]

The comparison to Houdon is interesting, if only because the French sculptor comes into play in Burke's story of how she came to model Roosevelt and ultimately claim credit for the dime's design.

'Then some'

Born in Mooresville, N.C., on Dec. 31, 1900, Burke gained her entrance to Roosevelt's inner sanctum by winning an art competition in 1943, sponsored by the Fine Arts Commission for the District of Columbia.

Burke was in a Staten Island, N.Y., hospital, recovering from a back injury sustained as a truck driver for the Navy, when she learned that she had won the competition, which called for

∗★∗

Burke's original drawing of President Franklin D. Roosevelt on brown butcher's paper.

her to prepare a profile of Roosevelt for a plaque to be placed in the Recorder of Deeds building in Washington, D.C. The notice that she won had been sent some time earlier but, as Burke was laid up with her injury, had gone unnoticed in her accumulating mail at her New York apartment.

A friend eventually checked her mail, and doctors worked to get her back on her feet so she could complete a design by the pre-set deadline. With the help of friends, she obtained several pictures of the president but found few that could be used.

"When I tried to find profiles of him, he was always with three-quarters of his face and smiling," Burke said. "So there weren't many profiles of him. I couldn't find [any] at that time. I had gone through all of the logs in the *New York Times*, every New York paper and every book.

"He was very popular and was photographed all over, but there was nothing that I could use that I saw. So I had to do a composite of what I thought he looked like in the first one.

President Harry S. Truman with Selma Burke, then 38, at the viewing of her plaque on Sept. 21, 1945, at the Recorder of Deeds building. Next to Burke is Marshall Shepard, recorder of deeds, whom she would later claim conspired with Mint engraver John Sinnock in Sinnock's using her design for the dime.

★★★

"But, my father had a saying: 'You have to do all you can and then some. It is the 'then some' that is going to get you where you want to go.'"[5]

Burke decided she hadn't done all she could, so she wrote to the president:

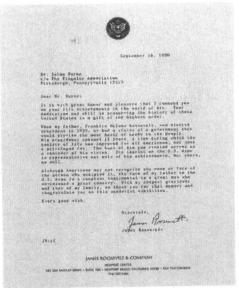

A Sept. 16, 1990, letter from Franklin D. Roosevelt's son James to Burke commending her for her artistic achievements, including the Roosevelt dime.

> ...[I] asked him if he would see me. I told him I was a student at Columbia and I had studied the background of Mr. Houdon, who was a French sculptor who had done the president, President Washington — the quarter that we have. And it took him [Houdon] two months to come to America...and that the best bust of Washington was done by Houdon.
>
> I said, 'You know, Mr. President, I am about four hours by train from Washington and I am two hours by plane.' And, I said, 'I have a Ford automobile and I could be down there in five or six hours in my Ford automobile if you would see me just for a few minutes so I could make some sketches.'

Roosevelt agreed to meet with her.

'Four Freedoms'

A model for sculptor Manship and others, Burke cut a stylish figure, arriving at the White House decked out in a grey-striped suit, sporting an umbrella and portfolio — an image interrupted only by a roll of brown butcher's paper she had acquired from an A&P grocery store on which to draw.

★★★

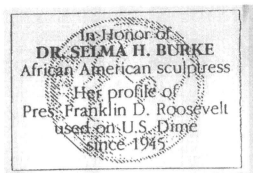

In Honor of
DR. SELMA H. BURKE
African American sculptress
Her profile of
Pres. Franklin D. Roosevelt
used on U.S. Dime
since 1945

Burke and others would give out dimes encased in a holder noting her role in the dime's design.

LURKING COMRADE

Did the "JRS" initials on the Franklin half dollar, released in 1948, stand for Joseph Stalin. No, they represented engraver John Sinnock.

In a version of this tall tale, a Communist was lurking in the Mint who secretly placed his comrade's initials on the coin.[1]

A colorful rumor had it that the U.S. dime carried the initials of Joseph Stalin, not John Sinnock.

"When I came in, he was sitting there, you know, in his wheelchair, and he had his hand out," she said of her first meeting with Roosevelt. "I thought I'd never get to it. Anyway, we shook hands and I started taking off my coat and putting down my things.

"I was just in a hurry, because he said he was going to give me 45 minutes and I wanted to use that 45 minutes making sketches. So I took off my things and threw everything off but my hat and I just started to draw him. In the meantime, he was asking me all of these questions... we just got on beautifully."

They talked about Roosevelt's home and shared a common acquaintance in Peace Mission movement leader Father Divine, who ran an inexpensive New York kitchen Burke frequented during her days of teaching art as part of the Work Progress Administration's efforts in Harlem.

"But all the time, I'm trying to talk to him and I am trying to draw...so that certain parts of his face were done well and certain parts were done badly," she said. "So I had to start over again.

★ ★ ★

Mint engraver John Sinnock.

That is when I got up and took his head and said, 'Would you just hold like this for a few minutes.'" Roosevelt did.

She would go back a second time and continue her modeling. Over the years of her acquaintance with Roosevelt, she collected 35 letters between her and the president, which she cherished and proudly displayed.

Burke also fondly remembered a visit from First Lady Eleanor Roosevelt on the morning of March 6, 1945. Mrs. Roosevelt had come to view the drawing.

✶★✶

Sinnock did his own studies of Franklin D. Roosevelt from life in the early 1930s, as shown by a Mint inaugural medal. The same Roosevelt portrait was used for this memorial medal issued by the Mint after the president's death.

★★★

Burke's sister made breakfast, using fine silver passed down through the family and originally received, Burke said, by her grandfather from Stonewall Jackson.

"And I had a card table, and my aunt had made a very, very beautiful little handmade tablecloth," Burke said. "My sister served cranberry juice; most people weren't drinking it then.

"We had the Roosevelt profile over on my easel. I had a special easel. So we pulled the cord and everybody went 'ah,' except Mrs. Roosevelt. She just kept looking and looking."

She told Burke that it looked like Roosevelt but complained, "You have made him very young."

"That is when I started giving her a lecture," Burke said. "I was much more of a professorial type then than I am now. I've learned to be gentle with people, no matter who they are."

She told Mrs. Roosevelt: "No, I've done it for tomorrow and tomorrow. I don't want the people [to] feel something about a wrinkled old man. I want to give the feeling of a strong Roman gladiator that we could feel was strong and would lead our country."

Mrs. Roosevelt asked Burke if she would like another sitting with the president. Burke agreed.

Plans were made for an additional 45 minutes of modeling to take place on April 20 while the president was in San Francisco

Our fascist dime

Lesser known from the rumor mill, but basically on the same level as the various Communist-infiltration tales attached to other U.S. coins, was the Mercury dime's supposed link to fascism. Even though the fasces (a Roman symbol of authority) were incorporated into Adolph Weinman's design long before the rise of fascism, the Mercury dime engendered criticism for its supposed reference to the hated ideology and Italy's ruler, Benito Mussolini.

Under the headline "He'll Find it There, All Right," the April 1926 issue of *The Numismatist* quotes from the *Chicago Evening Post*.

Anyone who denounces Mussolini for the adoption of a battle-ax as the symbol of the Fascisti, says Representative Sol Bloom, says, better take a look at a dime.[2]

The fasces, a Roman symbol of authority, was criticized when it was used for the Mercury dime.

★★★

attending a conference, but the president died before the meeting could occur.

The Mercury dime's fasces, on the coin's reverse, were a source of sarcasm. When the coin was released, in 1916, some termed it the "golf coin" because of the resemblance of the fasces to a golf club. Others called it the "battle ax" dime.

"So I never bothered the drawing anymore," she said. "I just finished that plaque, that relief, and had it in the show [at the Modern Age Gallery, July 1945]."

Her work on the drawing at the White House drew the attention of major magazines and newspapers, Burke said, including the *Washington Post*, *Time* and *Life*. But, she said, she shunned this because she wanted recognition for the finished work not her visits with the president.

She did receive notice in *Time* magazine for the drawing and again when the plaque was officially unveiled on Sept. 24, 1945.

President Harry S. Truman was on hand for the official dedication of the plaque, saying of her depiction of Roosevelt, "you got him as we knew him at his best."

Reporting on the unveiling, the Sept. 25, 1945, issue of the Washington, D.C. *Evening Star* said the $750 plaque, known as the *Four Freedoms*, had been commissioned by the District Commissioners in July 1943 for the new $450,000 Recorder of Deeds building at Sixth and D streets N.W. Ground for the structure had been broken in September 1940 by President Roosevelt.

The plaque was unveiled by Frederick S. Weaver, deputy recorder of deeds, great grandson of abolitionist Frederick Douglass. Douglass had served as the first black recorder of deeds in Washington, D.C., and as a district commissioner. The ceremony was presided over by Marshall L. Shepard, recorder of deeds, who explained that the plaque was the dream of Dr. William J. Tompkins, former recorder of deeds. Burke is shown in an Associated Press photograph with Truman, the plaque, and Shepard.

The ceremony featured speeches, radio vocalists, performances by the Metropolitan Police Band and the official presentation of the bronze *Four Freedoms* plaque by Rep. William L. Dawson, D-Ill., to Commissioner John Russell Young.[6]

★★★

Burke, the artist

This was the first in a string of major achievements in what was to be a long and distinguished art career that did not come to fruition until later in life. Burke first trained for a medical career and spent some time as a surgeon's technician at St. Agnes School of Nursing in Raleigh, N.C.

It was during a stint as a private nurse in a wealthy New York home in the late 1920s that she gained exposure to high culture, visiting the opera on numerous occasions with her wealthy employer and working as a model for such notables as Manship; Edward Steichen, a pioneer in photography as an art form; and Alfred Stieglitz, a prominent photo-engraver. It was these influences, she said, that eventually turned her attention to art.

In 1935 she won the Rosewald Foundation Fellowship. One year later she was awarded the Boehler Foundation Fellowship. The fellowships allowed her to travel to Europe, where she studied with French painter Henri Matisse and sculptor Aristide Maillol.

STARS AND BARS

First issues of the Shield nickel, released just after the end of the Civil War, displayed rays between the stars on the reverse. Some saw these "stars and bars" as representative of the Confederate battle flag — put there, they believed, to promote the defeated Southern cause.[3]

The design on the reverse of the 1866 Shield nickel featured stars and rays. The rays were removed the following year because of striking problems.

She left Europe a few months before Hitler invaded Austria and returned to New York where, in 1941, she earned a master's degree in fine arts from Columbia University.

In 1970, at the age of 70, she received a doctorate in arts and letters from Livingstone College, Salisbury, N.C. It is only one in a lengthy list of credits that included an additional doctorate, in teaching, and numerous honorary degrees.

Burke also founded the Selma Burke School of Sculpture in

★

New York and the Selma Burke Art Center in Pittsburgh. She was a recognized poet and had an algebra problem published in a major mathematics book.

RINGING THE BELL

The Liberty Bell appears on a number of U.S. coins. It was first shown on the 1926 Sesquicentennial of American Independence commemorative half dollar credited to John Sinnock, after a design by John Frederick Lewis. Next it was on the Franklin half dollar (1948-1963), and then it appeared on Dennis R. Williams' design for the reverse of the Bicentennial Eisenhower dollar.

The 1926 Sesquicentennial half dollar credited to John Sinnock.

Burke also lectured at Harvard, Swarthmore, Livingstone and other colleges and was singled out for her outstanding achievements by the governors of Pennsylvania and North Carolina. In Pennsylvania she was honored with the Distinguished Daughter of Pennsylvania award. Prior recipients included Princess Grace of Monaco, Pearl S. Buck and Mamie Eisenhower.

In October 1990 a major four-month exhibit of her works opened at the Lyndon Baines Johnson Library and Museum, part of the University of Texas, and was viewed by an estimated 90,000 people.

Among more than 1,000 of her sculptures gracing college campuses, museums and private collections is a moving bronze statue, *Uplift,* relating a disturbing scene of a mother and her children huddling close together during a lynching — a piece that links directly to Burke's past.

A bronze example of this statue was donated in 1991 to Hillship Township, W.Va., in honor of the 100th anniversary of the birth of Pulitzer Prize-winning author Pearl S. Buck. An additional version was presented to Spellman College in 1993.

Also by Burke are the *John Brown Memorial* in Lake Placid, N.Y., a bust of Booker T. Washington for the federal government, a bronze of Dr. Martin Luther King, and a bust of Duke Ellington.

★ ★ ★

Astronaut Edwin E. "Buz" Aldrin, Jr. on the surface of the moon during the Apollo 11 mission.

APOLLO 11 COIN

The reverses of the Eisenhower dollar (1971-1978) and the Susan B. Anthony dollar (1979-1999) share something in common. Both show a representation of a patch worn by Apollo 11 astronauts on their historic mission to the moon. Designed by Frank Gasparro and used for all years of issue except for 1975-1976, the reverse of the Eisenhower dollar (and later the Anthony dollar) has an eagle, representing the lunar landing module, the *Eagle*, landing on the moon's surface with the earth in the background.

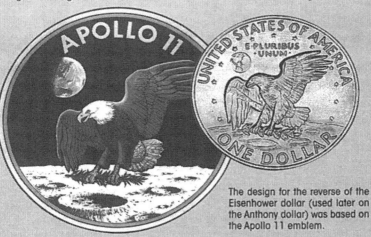

The design for the reverse of the Eisenhower dollar (used later on the Anthony dollar) was based on the Apollo 11 emblem.

High praise

A 1990-dated proclamation from Pennsylvania Gov. Robert P. Casey praised Burke, saying:

> You have had the opportunity to travel around the world studying under such world-famous artists as Henri Matisse and Reis. You have helped young people develop an appreciation for the arts. And your leadership and compassion for those you work with will continue to produce future artists.
>
> You have captured the essence of greatness, of sorrow, of love and of humanity in your works. Your sensitivity is evident in your statue of Dr. Martin Luther King Jr., the bronze bust of Duke Ellington, and the portrait of President Franklin D. Roosevelt.
>
> Your ten cents can be found in every community across the nation. But that dime is worth so much more than its monetary value. By sculpting President Roosevelt, you preserved for all time an artistic talent that reflects our history and, at the same time, generates pride in the African-American culture.

Another who praised her for work on the dime was FDR's son, James, who wrote to Burke on Sept. 16, 1990, from Newport Beach, Calif., saying:

EXTRA LEAVES

Typifying Wisconsin, the state quarter shows a cow, cheese and corn—three things this dairy state is known for. Not typical was the existence of "extra leaf" varieties that stirred up the hobby in 2005. Found were 2004-D Wisconsin quarters with an extra leaf to the left side of the cornhusk. These came in high- and low-leaf varieties.

The state quarter series was somewhat of a boon for variety collectors and roll searchers, as several issues were found with doubling, die cracks and other anomalies. Included among these were 2005 Minnesota quarters and 2005 Oregon quarters with doubling that appeared to add extra trees and branches and other remnants to the skylines. Also discovered were clash marks (remains of two dies coming together without a planchet between them) that look like fish in the water on a Minnesota quarter.

* ★ *

ALUMINUM RARITY

In the early 1970s, with copper prices causing problems, the Treasury considered a switch from copper to aluminum for the nation's one-cent piece. This led to the creation of patterns dated 1974 in aluminum (with more than 1.5 million reportedly struck to test the mechanics).

To help promote the idea, the Mint brought some of the aluminum patterns to Capitol Hill for congressmen to examine. And that's where things went wrong. The May 3, 1975, issue of *Numismatic News* reported that: "On April 22 [1975], a spokesman for the Bureau of the Mint verified that 16 of the 1974-dated patterns, which were struck in December, 1973, when the agency was considering a change in the Lincoln's cent's alloy, had been sent to Capitol Hill for study by members of the House and Senate banking committees, but only two of them had been returned. The rest have mysteriously disappeared." In 1976, the number brought to Capitol Hill was put at 15, not 16, and four of these were returned.

In 2001 an example was sent to the *News'* offices in Iola, Wis., where it was verified to be genuine. The story was that a Capital policeman, on duty in the basement of the House Office Building in late 1973, saw a coin he believed to be a dime lying on the floor and picked it up. The coin eventually ended up in the hands of one of his relatives, who submitted it to *Numismatic News* for examination. It weighed 0.93 grams as compared to 3.11 grams of a copper cent.

When my father, Franklin Delano Roosevelt, was elected president in 1933, he had a vision of a government that would provide the most basic of needs to its people. His presidency spanned 12 years, a time during which the quality of life was improved for all Americans, not just a privileged few. The bust of him you created serves as a reminder of his vision. Its imprint on the U.S. dime is representative not only of his achievements, but yours, as well.

Although Americans may not recognize the name or face of the person who sculpted it, the face of my father on the U.S. dime is a constant testimonial to a great man who envisioned a great country. With my deepest gratitude and that of my family, we thank you for that memory and congratulate you on this wonderful exhibition.

But even though governors, FDR's relatives and others of note came to accept Burke's claims of having designed the

★★★

dime, few within the numismatic world have credited her with doing so. Her story has appeared sporadically in numismatic circles over the years, with only limited support. Chief among those who have followed her background is Edward C. Rochette, a prolific numismatic writer and former American Numismatic Association president.

Rochette, who graciously provided his file of background material as reference, has argued in her favor. In a *Los Angeles Times* article, maintained as part of his file, he wrote of the modeling of the president:

> ...that [Burke's] image was soon to become the most prolifically issued image the world would know of FDR. To many, it was the portrait plagiarized by the U.S. Mint for the design of the Roosevelt dime.

> Some argue that Roosevelt's features are so distinctive that all profile portraits of the president will be similar. Circumstantial or not, all one has to do is to compare the preliminary sketches prepared by Sinnock to the portrait on display at the Hall of Records.

> Sinnock's initial designs not only bore remarkable similarity, but his suggested reverse featured a representation of the Four Freedoms — not unlike that featured on Burke's plaque.

DATE FREEZE

The year 1964 was a long one, if you count the date freeze on U.S. coins. On Sept. 3, 1964, President Lyndon Johnson signed special legislation allowing the Treasury secretary to use the 1964 date on coins until he "determines that adequate supplies of coins are available." Faced with a coinage shortage, this took until April 1965.

Asking, "Did history repeat itself in 1945?", Rochette explained that it wouldn't be the first time Sinnock was charged with numismatic plagiarism.

In 1925 Mint employee Sinnock had submitted designs for the Sesquicentennial of Independence half dollar. The sponsoring commission rejected them and hired artist John Frederick Lewis to redesign the coin. Lewis' sketches were accepted by the Commission of Fine Arts and appear on the coin, which bears Sinnock's initials and makes no mention of Lewis.

★★★

Late night call

According to Burke, history did repeat itself. She said she received a call late one night from Ruth Wilson, a secretary at the Recorder of Deeds office, urging her to come to Washington, saying that her drawing was being sent to the Mint for use in designing the dime.

"The reason why I knew that Mr. Sinnock had gotten it from there was that Ruth Wilson had called me in the middle of the night, in New York, to tell me that this man, Sinnock, and Marshall Shepard were making a deal and that he had taken the drawing to the Mint," Burke said. "Ruth Wilson said, 'You'd better come

BETTER PLACEMENT

It wasn't a defect, but U.S. Mint Director F.J.H. von Engelken apparently thought the small mintmark on the obverses of the first Walking Liberty half dollars looked amiss. The mintmark for coins struck at Denver and San Francisco in 1916 was on the obverse only. For the 1917 coinage, it can be found on the obverse or the reverse. This is because, as disclosed by letters from the period, Von Engelken thought the placement of the letter below the date looked like a coinage defect. It wasn't, but during the production of the 1917 Walking Liberty halves his order that it be moved to the reverse took effect.

It would remain there for the rest of the coinage. As a result, mintages for the coins with the obverse mintmark were lower in 1917 than those with the mark on the reverse, and bring higher premiums.

A 1917 Walking Liberty half dollar with the mintmark on the obverse.

★★★

to Washington because Marshall Shepard and Sinnock are doing a thing on you.'"

According to Burke, Wilson and herself were godparents to the daughter of a Mary Wilson.

"She [Ruth Wilson] felt very close and she had to let me know what was going on," Burke said. "I was sleeping, and I said, 'I am not going to Washington. I won this thing.' No, I just took a stand."

OLD MAN CRASHES DOWN

Fortunately for New Hampshire, it has a 2000-dated state quarter depicting one of its most famed geographical features, the Old Man of the Mountain — a mountain outcropping in Franconia Notch that resembled the face of an old man, but which came crashing down on May 3, 2003.

Three years after the New Hampshire state quarter depicting the Old Man of the Mountain was released, the popular outcropping (shown below) came crashing down.

★★★

Burke also believed part of the reason she has never received full credit for the design was the politics of the period. She believed the change in administration from Democratic to Republican, which affected the leadership at the Recorder of Deeds office, had some impact on proper credit not being accorded to her. The plaque had been the idea of a Democrat to honor a Democrat president, and Shepard was a Republican.

"So I am sure that it was because there was no one watching what was going on," she said, "and because they found out I was black. That was definitely one of the things at that particular time. The material that I sent, when they let the competition, had nothing to do with race. I had done many white people.

"I was a student at Columbia and I did a bust of William Allen and of Charlie Schwab, the financier." It was, she said, such work that won her the commission, not her race.

Burke maintained that her subsequent attempts to gain credit for the dime led J. Edgar Hoover to launch an FBI investigation into her activities.

Not helping the cause, she said, was that she once carried a banner in a New York parade that advocated freedom of press and other civil liberties but was tagged by some as socialist in bent.

"My husband [Claude McKay] was a very well-known writer," Burke said. "And he said, 'Well, I don't want to get mixed up in that [communism], but I would sure like to march in that parade.' So I said, 'I'll march.'

"So I was in this communist parade from 14th Street to 59th Street carrying a banner, a big thing, 'I am for free press.' It was

CHEERIOS DOLLARS

Some who ate their Cheerios in 2000 were happy discover inside the box a new Sacagawea dollar that turned out to be a rare variety. As part of a promotion that year by General Mills, 5,500 2000-P Sacagawea dollars were randomly placed in 10 million boxes of Cheerios.

Some of the coins carried a reverse from pattern hubs. On those struck with dies made from the pattern hubs, the detail in the wing and tail feathers is more pronounced than on the regular strikes.

The variety wasn't discovered until 2005 and it has since been established that not all of the Cheerios boxes contained the valuable variety, some housed coins with the normal reverse.

* * *

the only way the newspapers could be in that parade, because they didn't want to get in a parade of communism to get their fight over.

"But I could, because I wasn't anything but just an ordinary citizen who wanted the press free. Everything was so separated and segregated that one didn't think about that communist thing."

Whether or not she became the target of an FBI investigation is largely a moot point when it comes to the story of the dime, though it framed some of her mind-set concerning whom she blamed for her drawing being used without proper attribution.

Interestingly, Hoover did at least once deny that Burke was under investigation. This was in response to an April 11, 1945, inquiry about the sculptor from Malvina C. Thompson, secretary to First Lady Eleanor Roosevelt, a copy of which appears in *Dear Mrs. Roosevelt: Letters to Eleanor Roosevelt through Depression and War* edited by Cathy D. Knepper, Ph.D. (Carroll & Graf Publishers, New York, 2004.)

> ### ALSO COLLECTIBLE
>
> U.S. collectors can also look to add coins to their collections issued by Hawaii, when it was a kingdom (1883 dime, quarter, half dollar and dollar of King Kalakaua I) and an 1847 cent of King Kamehameha III among the official issues, and coins of the Philippines under the sovereignty of the United States (including half, one, five 10, 20, 50 centavos and one-peso pieces beginning in 1903) and commonwealth issues beginning in 1937. The Philippines became an independent republic in 1946.

The letters assembled by Dr. Knepper include one from a Kathryn Churchill, who signed her missive as a flower consultant from New York City and included a clip from a column by Eleanor Roosevelt in which the First Lady wrote that she had been to Burke's studio to view Burke's depiction of Franklin D. Roosevelt. In the March 8, 1945, letter (appearing on p. 339 of Knepper's book), Churchill wrote to the First Lady that she was surprised that Burke was working on a depiction of the president, as Burke, according to Churchill, had been investigated by the FBI for her activities in 1940 when Burke was living in New York as the wife of a German spy and active in New Jersey bunds. Hoover responded in a letter (reproduced on p. 342 of Knepper's work) that there was no negative information in the FBI's files about Burke, but her German intimate was investigated, but no evidence of espionage was found and the investigation was dropped.

⋆★⋆

Open to question

Legitimate arguments can also be offered in rebuttal to Burke's claim. For instance, just because Sinnock has been charged with artistic plagiarism in regard to the 1926 Sesquicentennial half dollar doesn't automatically condemn him in relation to the dime.

An article in the March 1946 issue of *Numismatic Scrapbook Magazine* says Sinnock claimed to have used two life-studies he did of Roosevelt during 1933-1934 for the dime and consulted photos of the president.[7]

Sinnock did prepare studies of Roosevelt from life during the time period mentioned. The results are shown on a Mint inaugural medal issued in 1933.

The medal depicts Roosevelt's profile facing right, not left as on the dime, but bears a similarity. Above all, it suggests that Sinnock had his own studies to draw upon in preparation of the dime and leads one to wonder why he would need to plagiarize another artist's work.

If, however, as Rochette contends, Burke's image of Roosevelt was widely known, it's not inconceivable that Sinnock arranged to have her drawing sent over for study. There's just no solid proof that he did. Letters from Roosevelt's relatives and others thanking Burke for her work on the dime are treasures and show that others supported her claim, but cannot go far enough to fully substantiate it. The principals who could, including Ruth Wilson, have long since died.

The door cannot be summarily closed on her story, but the passage of time has made it nearly impossible to jar it open. That Burke was a gifted sculptor, artist, and a remarkable woman cannot be denied. That her drawing of Roosevelt played a role in history is also without doubt. That it had a role in the dime's design will, however, likely always remain open to question.

★★★

One of the errant tales about the rarity of the 1804 silver dollars was that they went to a watery grave when Navy Lt. Stephen Decatur set the *Philadelphia* aflame.

Chapter 22

An Unsinkable Coin

The frigate *Philadelphia* shown entering Tripoli harbor.

$\mathbf{S}$hipwrecks are a popular source of riches for today's treasure hunter. They should also be a popular source for 1804 silver dollars, if you believe the rumors circulated for years as explanation for this coin being a great U.S. rarity.

Though not the only coin ever touted as having come by its rarity via its mintage being vanquished to Davy Jones' locker, the 1804 dollar is one of the most famous and valuable of U.S. coins, bringing with it tall tales fit for any swashbuckler worth his sea salt.

⋆★⋆

Miscalculations in the proper weight for the U.S. silver dollar, first struck in 1794, led to the coins being produced primarily for export. Few entered circulation, and coinage was stopped.

Creating a rarity

Coinage of the silver dollar began at the U.S. Mint in 1794, but miscalculations as to the proper weight for the coin caused the coins to disappear from circulation soon after release.

A depositor at the first Mint could make a profit at the Mint's expense by sending the coins to the West Indies. There, the lighter-weight U.S. silver dollars were traded at par for the heavier Spanish or Mexican eight reales, which were shipped back to the United States for recoinage. As a result, few early U.S. silver dollars entered circulation, most were melted.

The same story was basically true for the nation's early gold coinage. The bimetallic ratio set by the United States, by which silver traded for gold, was at first off the mark in relation to world ratios. This meant that gold coins either disappeared shortly after minting or languished in bank vaults.

It is generally agreed today that no U.S. silver dollars dated 1804 were struck. In that year, coinage had been halted because of the inability to keep the coins in circulation.

Landmark research by Eric P. Newman and Kenneth E. Bressett, presented in their 1962 book *The Fantastic 1804 Silver Dollar,* has convinced numismatists that the 19,570 silver dollars recorded by the Mint as being struck in 1804 were actually dated

★★★

1803. Further, that the first known examples of 1804-dated silver dollars (Class I) were minted in the 1830s for inclusion in special presentation sets to be given to foreign dignitaries. Additional strikings were made surreptitiously through the latter part of the 19th century. Today the count stands at 15 genuine examples known and hundreds, if not thousands, of fakes.

Seaworthy tales

Until the Newman and Bressett book, numismatists were informally divided into two groups — those who believed existing 1804 dollars were struck in 1804 and those who thought the coins were of later manufacture.

To explain how these coins could have been minted in 1804, several tales of high-seas adventure surfaced. One of the more spirited was tied to the Barbary Coast pirates.

Under this history-soaked tale, the coins went to a watery grave aboard the U.S. frigate *Philadelphia*. The frigate was set aflame in February 1804 by Navy Lt. Stephen Decatur, who heroically sailed the ketch *Intrepid* into Tripoli harbor to keep the *Philadelphia* out of the hands of the Tripolitanians. Most of the 1804 dollar and half dollar mintage went down, like any good captain, with the ship.

Newman and Bressett tell an additional Tripoli-related tale, by which, in 1804 an expedition was led from the United States against Tripoli, headed by Capt. William Eaton and Hamet Carmanly, the exiled brother of the bashaw of Tripoli. After 15 days of torturous marching across thousands of miles of searing desert, they accomplished their mission. The 1804 silver dollars were shipped to the coast of Africa to pay the brave men. Few of the rare dollars ever returned to this country.[1]

Oriental misadventure

Yet another seagoing theory placed the coins in an iron chest aboard a merchantman bound for a U.S. frigate in Oriental waters. The victim of a typhoon, the merchantman and its precious cargo went to the bottom of the stormy sea.[2]

In a different version, by which all but a few of the 1804 dollars "now lie at the bottom of the Pacific ocean somewhere between Cape Horn and Hong-Kong," religious zealots were blamed. Apparently a Huguenot employed at the Mint was the culprit. He

★

Although dated 1804, no silver dollars were struck in that year with that date. The first of the 1804 silver dollars were produced in the 1830s, with later strikings bringing the number known to 15. The piece shown is the Class I Dexter specimen.

became incensed by the portrait of the silver dollar, believing it bore too close a resemblance to First Lady Martha Washington. He let the word out to others, and Huguenots throughout the nation "set up a hue and cry against having the picture of any ruler or any member of any ruler's or former ruler's family on the money. As a result, not one of the coins was sent from the mint for general distribution. A few of them afterward were traded by the mint for perfect specimens of coins that were not in the mint cabinet, and that accounts for the fact that just a few of them are in the hands of coin collectors."[3]

Land-based theories

Land-based theories for the disappearance of the 1804 silver dollars were also generously provided. One of the more plausible asserted that the high price of silver caused the melting of most of the coinage. Another accounted for the low number of known examples by suggesting that the Mint had supplied just enough silver for 10 or 12 of the coins to be struck.[4]

Yet another theory, advanced by Robert E. Preston, U.S. Mint director 1893-1898, proclaimed that the entire mintage had been sent to Central America and only a few drifted back into this country.[5]

⋆✯⋆

Plenty of fakes

Ever since pioneer U.S. coin collector Matthew Stickney obtained an 1804 silver dollar in trade at the U.S. Mint in 1843, the 1804 silver dollar has been popular among collectors and perhaps even more popular with counterfeiters looking to make a quick buck. In the mid-1800s the nation's tavern keepers were targets for the unscrupulous, who fobbed off altered 1800-dated dollars as 1804 dollars.

B.H. Collins, described as having been associated with the U.S. Treasury for years, recorded in the March 1899 issue of *The Numismatist* that the bogus rarities were manufactured by a man named Kennedy in Lowell, Mass., who took 1800-dated dollars, removed the final "0." "covered the face [of the coin] with wax, etched a figure 4 in the proper place" and, with the use of a galvanic battery, attached the new digit in such a means that it "endured all the tests known to numismatics."

The famed King of Siam proof set, prepared in 1834 for presentation as a diplomatic gift and including rarities of the 1834 coinage, the famed 1804 gold $10 and the 1804 silver dollar.

★★★

Unlike the 1804 silver dollar, a small number of 1804-dated gold $10s were struck before the official order came to halt eagle and silver dollar coinage. Like the 1804 silver dollars, a limited number of 1804-dated gold $10s were produced in the 1830s for inclusion in diplomatic presentation sets. Only four of these "plain 4" proofs are known. Originals had a "crosslet 4" in the date.

The newly created 1804 dollars were then distributed by tramps in his employ, "who claimed to have inherited fortunes and wasted them in dissipation, with the exception of one valuable coin, which was worth thousands of dollars."[6] With genuine 1804 silver dollars bringing in the range of $600 in the 1870s, it was likely a lucrative business.

Since then the population of known examples would at first glance appear to have grown considerably, as journals devoted to numismatics in the 20th century are littered with references to so-called "discoveries" of additional 1804 silver dollars. Most of these reports were ill-based. Only 15 genuine pieces of the three different classes of 1804 dollars are known, and it would take a king's ransom to purchase an example of the "King of American Coins," the unsinkable 1804 silver dollar.

★★★

Chapter 23

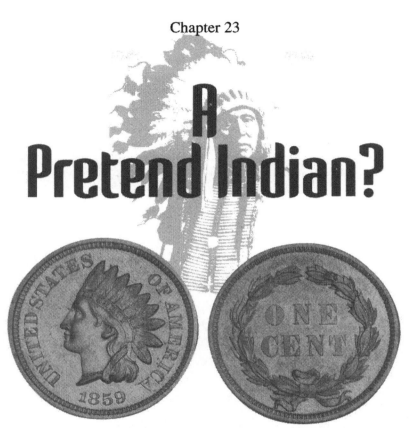

A Pretend Indian?

Coinage of the Indian Head cent began in 1859. It was designed by Mint engraver James B. Longacre and was long rumored to have been modeled after his young daughter, Sarah.

*C*ents have always been popular with collectors. This is especially true of the Indian Head cent, struck for circulation from 1859 into 1909.

For history buffs, it evokes images of the Old West via its Liberty adorned with an Indian headdress. For others, it is a reminder of a cheerful tale of a young girl, and an Indian chief and a loving father who placed her likeness on a U.S. coin for all to admire.

Alas, though, like so many other tales, it's a story entrenched primarily in numismatic lore.

★★★

A bit of malarkey

"It was a bright, sunny morning in 1835 when a group of Indians, who had been in Washington, D.C., to visit the Great White Chief, stopped by the U.S. Mint in Philadelphia. Their visit came just as James B. Longacre (Mint chief engraver 1828-1840) was showing his 12-year-old daughter, Sara, the workings of the Mint.

"An old chief, attracted by the sweet-faced maiden who had taken an interest in his Indian Headdress, placed the warbonnet on the young girl's head. It was such a striking picture that Longacre immediately took up sketch pad and began to draw his daughter in her borrowed headgear.

"The proud father, having previously entered a design competition for the new cent, and having racked his brain for an original and singular design with which to impress the judges, thought to himself that perhaps the combination of the Indian headfeathers and Saxon sweetness could win the prize.

"He submitted the drawing, surviving through several rounds of competition to finally have his design selected, winning the competition by one vote over more than 1,000 entries. Thus, his young daughter came to be immortalized on the nation's humblest of coins."

The sepia drawing of Sarah Longacre.

★★★

This bit of malarkey isn't quoted directly from anywhere, though it is a condensed version of a nonsensical story that appeared in a major numismatic publication quite some time ago. It can't be certain where the author got his penchant for spicing his story with liberal doses of pure imagination, though he claimed to be quoting directly from a Longacre relative. If he was, well, there's this bridge in Brooklyn, you see, and it's real, real cheap.

First, there was no competition for the design of the Indian Head cent. Mint chief engraver James B. Longacre designed it, plain and simple. Second, the coin wasn't released until 1859, 24 years after this story takes place. Third, Longacre's term at the Mint wasn't 1828-1840, rather 1844-1869.

Yet even within this fanciful tale there lies a bit of the problem that seemingly plagues numismatists at every turn — a "good story" has become so intermixed with the facts that it's hard to tell what's true anymore.

Relative memories

Even though the account above is seething with flaws, it was not the only instance in which a Longacre relative told of a visit by American Indians to James B. Longacre's home or the U.S. Mint (generally between 1844 and 1849), where young Sarah Longacre (most often age 12, sometimes 6, sometimes 16), posed for her father in an Indian headdress, inspiring his design for the Indian Head cent.

One of those versions was provided in the November 1931 issue of *The Numismatist*. It quoted a press dispatch from Falls City, Neb., saying:

> Add to your list of famous 'debunkers' Mrs. Sarah Peck, ninety-one-year old resident of this city. For those Americans who believe the feather bedecked head which appears on the Indian penny is that of some Indian, Mrs. Peck has this information:
>
> "The 'chief' was not an Indian at all. The picture is that of a little white girl, Mrs. Sarah Longacre Keen, a distant relative of Mrs. Peck.
>
> "As a girl of 12 Mrs. Keen visited her father at the United States Mint at Philadelphia, where he was employed as chief engraver. A competition was on

***

for sketches for the design of the new copper cent.

"A number of Indians, with their chief, visited the mint. The chief let the little girl wear his headgear. The effect was so striking that the father made a sketch, submitted it in the competition and won the award."[1]

Casting aspersions

Those who cast aspersions on this old family tale will tell you that the Indian Head cent's design is largely a repeat of that appearing on the gold dollars beginning in 1849, the double eagle of the same year, and later employed, in 1854, on the gold $3 piece. They'll also tell you correctly that Longacre once denied having used his daughter as a model.

One of the first to question the tale's validity was Mint chief engraver Charles Barber. In an article for *Sunset Magazine,* published shortly after coinage of the Indian Head cent had ended, Barber observed that it was hard to disprove a story of this kind. Most people, he said, "do not want any evidence to upset a pretty romance such as is now woven around this coin, any more than they are anxious for fact that will cast doubt upon the origin of our flag and the Betsy Ross romance."[2]

Barber added that although it was impossible at that late date (1910) to prove what Longacre used as a model, there was sufficient evidence "to satisfy an unprejudiced mind that he did not use either his daughter or an Indian war bonnet."[3]

Barber's source in this determination was a Mint employee, who, he said, remembered distinctly Longacre's sentiments regarding portraits on coins and that the engraver would have opposed using his daughter. The Mint employee, Barber said, also remembered that it was also Longacre's aim to portray an "ideal head" of an Indian female.

More striking, Barber claimed, is that the features of Liberty on the 1849 double eagle are the same as the cent.

"Now, if the child was only six years old in 1859 when the cent was executed, she certainly was not used for the model head in 1849," he wrote.[4] It was inconceivable to Barber that anyone looking at the Liberty on the cent could believe the features were those of a six-year-old girl or even a young girl."[5]

* * *

Those who dispute the story of Sarah Longacre's modeling for her father's coin contend the depiction of Liberty on the cent is the same as the Liberty James B. Longacre created for the gold dollar, gold $3 and the gold $20.

James B. Longacre wrote of the double eagle that it corresponded to the *Venus Accroupie* (or Crouching Venus).

★★★

The same basic head, Barber said, is found on the $3 gold coin and on a pattern coin with a seated figure. He complained that it was apparently incomprehensible to most people that an artist working on the design of a head or face "has not the most remote idea of making a portrait," even though he may have used a model.

Barber added:

> We have heard it said many times, all of which is untrue, that the Longacre head upon the double eagle was his wife's, that the head upon the standard dollar is that of a Philadelphia school teacher, that the head upon the rare eagle is a portrait of an Irish girl in the employ of Mr. Saint-Gaudens. Although, Homer Saint-Gaudens, the artist's son, tells us the latter was a study for the Victory of the Sherman statue.[6]

As for the Indian headdress, Barber said the feathers in the cent's design are not those of a warbonnet and could not have been sketched from any real bonnet taken from any head of any Indian.

Numismatic author Walter Breen also questioned the story behind Sara Longacre's posing for the Indian Head cent.

In the April 1951 issue of *Numismatic Scrapbook Magazine* Breen wrote that the debate could be laid to rest by the records of the National Archives.

According to Breen, Longacre planned to apply the head designed for the gold dollar in 1849 to other denominations, except the double eagle. Of the double eagle, Longacre wrote in a letter to the Treasury secretary, "The entire design, arrangement and execution are my own — the artistic proportions of the head are from antiquity, and will be found to correspond very nearly with those of the **Venus Accroupie,** a favorite standard."[7]

Breen determined that in no way was Longacre portraying any individual rather than a Hellenic pattern, the same as he did for the $3 gold piece.

Breen also quotes a Nov. 4, 1858, letter from Mint Director James Ross Snowden to Treasury Secretary Howell Cobb in which Snowden says the obverse shows "an ideal head of America — the drooping plumes of the North American Indian giving it the character of North America."[8]

★★★

In conclusion, Breen wrote, "in no case was anything but an ideal head of Liberty intended. The coin was based squarely on the classical profiles of ancient sculpture."

In a 1968 article for *Coins* magazine Breen said similarly:

> Suffice it to say that the head [on the $3 gold coin] does not depict any Indian, but rather (even as with the other gold) a Greco-Roman statue, probably the same Venus Acroupie which Longacre used ever since 1849. The three drawings reproduced here, as presented in [Don] Taxay's previously mentioned work, plainly prove that one and same engraving of a statue — and no Indian, nor yet Sarah Longacre, who was not even out of swaddling clothes in 1849 when Longacre first created this profile — served as the source for the Liberty heads Longacre put on gold and the 'Indian' head he put on the cent.[9]

Relative questions

Even with the detractors, and a denial by Longacre, the stories continued, largely propagated by Longacre's descendents, who insisted that the basis of the tale was true, even if the particulars were a bit messed up.

Comparison of Hellenistic Venus to the gold $3 and the Indian Head cent.

★★★

For example, grandson Rev. Lindsay B. Longacre took exception to the Breen article, writing in the November 1951 issue of *Numismatic Scrapbook Magazine* that although it was not impossible that the story behind the visit of the Indians was fabricated, it could also have been based on fact.[10]

Lindsay Longacre wrote that from childhood he knew James Longacre's daughter Sarah, as his Aunt Sallie. His father often told him the story of a "commission of Indians" who came to Washington on government business. Two of them visited with his grandfather at Longacre's home in Philadelphia. They laid aside their headdresses and Sallie picked one up, putting it on her head. Longacre then sketched her.

Lindsay Longacre maintained that the coin was idealized from this sketch. This story, he said, did not preclude the use of a classical ideal, as Breen had argued, nor did it necessitate an actual portrait.

Additional support

Cent specialist Rick Snow also found support for the theory that Sarah Longacre may have served as the inspiration for her father's coinage design.

In his book *Flying Eagle and Indian Cents,* Snow said a sepia of Sarah Longacre by her father, circa 1840, compares favorably to the design on the coin.

According to Snow, the sepia matches a later sketch of Sarah Longacre found in Longacre's sketchbook. The same sketchbook, Snow said, also contains Longacre's "other small cent sketches, including the Indian Cent prototype sketches."[11] Snow wrote:

> The most noticeable feature is the 'Longacre nose' whose profile runs straight from the tip to the forehead. The eyebrows, lips, and chin shape are very similar on all these sketches.[12]

He also contended that the Indian Head cent's depiction was not based on the design for the $20 gold piece and the $3 piece, but bears different features from those coins. The $20 and the $3 coins, he wrote, may indeed have been modeled after the Italian statue *Venus Accroupie* (or "Crouching Venus") as Breen suggested. The cent, he said, was not.

* ✸ *

End Notes

Chapter 1: Mistaken Identity

1. Although the traditionally quoted number of "missing" models is one, Fraser wrote in an undated letter to George E. Roberts, Mint director (1889-1907, 1910-1914), that: "Before the nickel was made I had done several portraits of Indians, among these Iron Tail, Two Moons and one or *two* [italics added] others, and probably got characteristics from those men in the heads on the coins, but my purpose was not to make a portrait but a type."

2. W. H. De Shon, "The New Five-Cent Piece," *The Numismatist*, May 1913, p. 239.

3. "The New Five Cent Piece," *The Numismatist*, March 1913, p. 130.

4. Undated letter from Fraser to Roberts.

5. See, for example, Elmo Scott Watson (titled through use of photos) "From Now on You'll be Seeing [Monticello and Jefferson] on Your Nickels, in Place of [Indian and bison]," Shelby, Mich. *Oceana Herald,* 4 March 1938.

6. Ibid.

7. Marianne F. Miller, "Buffaloed by the Buffalo Nickel," *Numismatic Scrapbook Magazine,* October 1956, p. 1697.

8. Ibid., p. 1703.

9. Ibid.

10. Leonard J. Ratzman, "The Buffalo Nickel, A 50-Year-Old Mystery," *Whitman Numismatic Journal,* June 1964, p. 27.

11. "The Head on the Current Nickel," *The Numismatist,* July 1931, p. 485.

12. Ratzman, p. 28.

13. Ibid., p. 29.

14. Ibid., p. 31. The obituary notice circulated by the Associated Press at the time of the chief's death in 1967 states that John Big Tree once told a correspondent that he received $1.50 an hour for a three-hour sitting for Fraser.

15. See "The Most Famous Coin" Famous Buffalo Nickel Only One of James E. Fraser's Great Works," *Coin World,* 23 December 1964, pp. 48, 54, 70. Reprint of article from Spring 1957 issue of *News From the Front,* a publication of the Home Insurance Co., New York, N.Y., edited by Kenneth Dunshee.

16. Alice Glaser, "The Indian-Head Nickel: Some Words With Himself... About the Wild West, the Pontiac, and the Last of the Seneca Chiefs," *Esquire,* March 1964.

17. Ibid.

18. Annette R. Cohen and Ray M. Druley, *The Buffalo Nickel* (Arlington, Va.: Potomac Enterprises, 1979), pp. 18-19.

19. In the *Coin World* reprint of the article from Home Insurance Co.'s Spring 1957 issue of *News From the Front* the author (likely Kenneth Dunshee) notes: "Recently, however, Mrs. Laura Gardin Fraser did

★★★

recall to the present writer that the third Indian had been Big Tree, a Kiowa, who was a favorite model of Fraser on several occasions."

20. Norman C. Davis, *The Complete Book of United States Coin Collecting* (New York: Mcmillan Publishing, 1971; revised ed., New York: Mcmillan Publishing, 1976), p. 69.
21. Lee Martin, *Coin Columns* (Anaheim, Calif.: Clarke Printing, Anaheim, Calif., 1966), p. 59.
22. "Chief John Big Tree the Man on the Buffalo Nickel Highlights 1966 TNA Convention," *Numismatic News*, 25 April 1966, p. 16.
23. Dean Krakel, *End of the Trail: The Odyssey of a Statue* (Norman, Okla.: University of Oklahoma Press, 1973), p. 26.
24. Ibid.
25. Krakel links Fraser's comments to an interview. Ratzman, however, provides the same quote concerning Fraser's "objective," but ascribes its source to a letter of explanation from Fraser to the Mint. The quote concerning the Indian models could hail from the same unidentified source.
    The same quotes used by Krakel also appear in William Bridges, *Gathering of Animals: An Unconventional History of the New York Zoological Society* (New York: Harper and Row, 1974), p. 146, but without attribution. The New York Zoological Society, or Bronx Zoo, is often said to have been the site where Black Diamond, the bison named by Fraser as the model for the reverse of the Indian Head nickel, was held. Bridges was curator of publications for the society and did extensive research into the zoo's early history.
26. See John W. Dunn, "Silent Warwhoop Muffled Hooves," *Coins*, December 1973, pp. 64-65.
27. "The New Five Cent Piece," *The Numismatist*, March 1913, p. 130.

Chapter 2: Buffaloed
1. Dean Krakel, *End of the Trail: The Odyssey of a Statue* (Norman, Okla.: University of Oklahoma Press, 1973), p. 26. Krakel was director of the Cowboy Hall of Fame in Oklahoma City, Okla., and involved in a project to restore an original example of Fraser's *End of the Trail* statue. The quote is misattributed by Krakel to an article by syndicated writer Elmo Scott Watson, which appeared in the 4 March 1938 issue of the Shelby, Mich. *Oceana Herald.* The same quotes appear in William Bridges, *Gathering of Animals: An Unconventional History of the New York Zoological Society* (New York: Harper and Row, 1974), p. 146, but without attribution. Similar quotes are also found in 27 January 1913 *New York Herald* and in John W. Dunn, "Silent Warwhoop Muffled Hooves," *Coins*, December 1973, pp. 64-65. Dunn wrote:
   "There has been much speculation over why and how James Earle Fraser used the portrait of an Indian on the obverse and a buffalo or bison on the reverse of the proposed five-cent coin. As a boy in South Dakota, Fraser had seen buffalo. He actually used for his model Black Diamond, who had been born in the Central Park Zoo in 1893 and was a prime attraction. In 1912, Fraser lived in New

★

York City not too far from the zoo and often sketched Black Diamond, because buffalo were considered very difficult to draw. Fraser often told the story that he desired to sketch Black Diamond in profile, but the shaggy animal always wanted to face the artist. Fraser had to pay the zoo attendant to attract Black Diamond's attention so that he could sketch the animal in profile."

2. Bridges, p. 146.
3. "Black Diamond is No More," *The Numismatist*, December 1915, p. 435.
4. Bridges, p. 71.
5. Ibid, p. 147.
6. Ibid.
7. Marianne F. Miller, in "A Sequel to the Buffalo Nickel," *Numismatic Scrapbook Magazine*, April 1957, tells a slightly different story. Quoting from an article by G.G. Goodwin, associate curator of the American Museum of Natural History, in a 1952 issue of *Natural History Magazine*, she reports that Charles R. Knight "was in the Zoological Museum in Washington when he spotted a man sketching a bull bison from a group that had been mounted at a request of W.T. Hornaday. Being an artist himself, he strolled over to see how the man was progressing. He found the man to be Mr. Baldwin, a Washington engraver, who was going to use the sketch for a buffalo note design. Mr. Knight offered to attempt the drawing, and much to his surprise, the offer was accepted. He decided, however, 'to use a living model instead of a stuffed one.' The article in the *Natural History Magazine* states, `This incident probably gave rise to the erroneous report that the buffalo on the nickel was taken from a large bull killed by Hornaday in Montana and mounted for the National Museum.' This certainly gives a logical explanation for the mixed-up buffaloes."
8. Bridges, p. 148.
9. "The New Five-Cent Piece," *The Numismatist*, March 1913, p. 131.
10. Bridges, p. 149.
11. "Buffalo-Nickel Buffalo Deposed as Herd Leader," *The Numismatist*, August 1926, p. 441.

Sidebars
1. "The New Fifty-Cent Piece," *Mehl's Numismatic Monthly*, February 1917, p. 20.

Chapter 3: An Orphaned Dime
1. Walter Breen, *Walter Breen's Complete Encyclopedia of U.S. and Colonial Coins* (New York: F.C.I. Press, Doubleday, 1987), p. 311. Breen contends that Ross, a "hack writer from the Kansas City area," hoarded the dimes, which are rare only in mint state.
2. See Frank C. Ross, "'Orphan Annie' (1844 Dime)," *Numismatic Scrapbook Magazine*, February 1946, p. 243.
3. See, for example, Bill The Coin Man, "'Little Orphan Annie' 1844 Dimes," *The Numismatist*, October 1935, p. 699, and the first edition of A *Guide Book of United States Coins* (Racine, Wis.: Whitman Publishing Co., 1947).

⋆★⋆

Sidebars
1. "Notes and Queries: Has a Lot of Trouble -" *The Numismatist,* May 1945, p. 450.

Chapter 4: Made in America
Sidebars
1. "A Comment on 1922 'Plain' Cent," *Numismatic Scrapbook Magazine,* July 1964, p. 1860.
2. "'Pennies From Heaven' in 1922," *The Numismatist,* July 1937, p. 645.
3. "An Automobile for Four Mint Marks (?)," *Mehl's Numismatic Monthly,* January 1915, p. 194.
4. Ibid., p. 195.

Chapter 6: A QuestionablePast
1. R.W. Julian, "Coin of Chance, Coin of Change, Coin of Conspiracy," *Coins,* May 1975, p. 69.
2. "Notes on the Convention," *The Numismatist,* October 1920, p. 466.
3. "The Rare 1913 Nickel," *The Numismatist,* January 1921, p. 17.
4. Julian, p. 70.
5. Ibid., p. 69.
6. "Deaths: Samuel W. Brown," *The Numismatist,* August 1944, p. 707. Brown was ANA member No. 808.
7. "Liberty 1913 Nickel Story Footnotes," *Numismatic Scrapbook Magazine,* April 1973, p. 372.
8. Arthur H. Lewis, *The Day They Shook the Plum Tree* (New York: Harcourt, Brace & World Inc., 1963), p. 247.
9. "Identifying 1913 Lib. Nickels," *Numismatic Scrapbook Magazine,* June 1961, p. 1709.
10. Abe Kosoff, *Abe Kosoff Remembers...50 Years of Numismatic Reflections,* New York: Sanford J. Durst Numismatic Publications, 1981), p. 76.
11. Ibid, p. 75.
12. Interview with Tom Fruit, 1993. Same for later quotations.
13. J.V. McDermott, "The Fabulous $50,000 Nickel," *Coins,* September 1966, p. 53. McDermott adds that he couldn't bring himself to dismiss another of the story's theories — that a guard let go in 1918 for unknown reasons had found the dies and struck examples.
14. "Obituaries: J.V. McDermott A.N.A. LM 135," *The Numismatist,* December 1966, p. 1640.

Sidebars
1. "The 'Phoney' Fake or Racketeer Nickel," *Numismatic Scrapbook Magazine,* May 1960, p. 1557.
2. Lester V. Berrey and Melvin Van Den Bark, *The American Thesaurus of Slang,* 2nd ed., (New York: Thomas Y. Crowell Co., New York, 1953), p. 878.

★

Chapter 7: Religious motto

1. "History of the Motto 'In God We Trust,' " U.S. Department of Treasury, *Twenty-Fourth Annual Report of the Director of the Mint to the Secretary of the Treasury for the Fiscal Year Ended June 30, 1896* (Washington, D.C.: Government Printing Office, 1897), p. 106.
2. Ibid. pp. 106-107.
3. Ibid., p. 107.
4. Homer Saint-Gaudens, "Roosevelt and Our Coin Designs: Letters Between Theodore Roosevelt and Augustus Saint-Gaudens," *The Century Illustrated Monthly Magazine* April 1920, p. 727.
5. Ibid.
6. Ibid.
7. Ibid, p. 728.
8. Letter from Theodore Roosevelt datelined Washington, Nov. 13, reprinted under "The Beginnings of Reform in Our Coinage," *The Numismatist,* January 1908.

Chapter 8: A Perfect Model

1. John H. Dryfhout, *The Work of Augustus Saint-Gaudens,* (Hanover, N.H.: University Press of New England, 1982), pp. 253-254.
2. Ibid., p. 35.
3. Homer Saint-Gaudens, "Roosevelt and Our Coin Designs: Letters Between Theodore Roosevelt and Augustus Saint-Gaudens," *Century Illustrated Monthly Magazine,* April 1920, p. 725.
4. Ibid.
5. Ibid.
6. Ibid.
7. Ibid., p. 726.
8. Ibid.
9. Weinman Papers, Archive of American Art, discovered by William E. Hagans.
10. Henry Hering, "History of the $10 and $20 Gold Coins of 1907 Issue," *The Numismatist,* August 1949, p. 455.
11. Ibid.
12. Ibid., p. 456.
13. Ibid.
14. Ibid.
15. "Want Native Face on Coin," *The Numismatist,* October-November 1907, p. 313.
16. William E. Hagans, "Author Contends Black Lady Modeled for Double Eagle," *Numismatic News,* 26 February 1991, p. 54.
17. Ibid.
18. Dryfhout, p. 219.
19. Burke Wilkinson makes a similar charge in *Uncommon Clay: The Life and Works of Augustus Saint-Gaudens* in relation to Homer Saint-Gaudens' attempt to obscure the memory of Augustus Saint-Gaudens' model and mistress, Davida Clark. Clark bore Saint-Gaudens' illegitimate son, Louis P. Clark.

* ★ *

20. Hagans, p. 54.
21. Ibid., p. 55.
22. Ibid.
23. Ibid.
24. Ibid.
25. Homer Saint-Gaudens, p. 733.
26. Adolph Weinman, Weinman Papers, Archive of American Art, discovered by William E. Hagans.
27. Hagans, p. 56.
28. Ibid., p. 55.

Sidebars

1. "The New Fifty-Cent Piece," *Mehl's Numismatic Monthly,* February 1917, p. 20.

Chapter 12: It's Not a 'Penny'

1. Walter Breen, *Complete Encyclopedia,* p. 216.

Chapter 13: Million Dollar Exhibit

Sidebars

1. "The New Peace Coin Now in Circulation: Proposed by Mr. Zerbe and Fathered by the A.N.A., the Standard Silver Dollar Now Appears With New Designs," *The Numismatist,* February 1922, p. 63.
2. Ibid.

Chapter 15: No More Trades

Sidebars

1. "No Change to be Made in Design of the Peace Dollar," *The Numismatist,* March 1922, p. 129.
2. Ibid.

Chapter 17: Roll Craze

Sidebars

1. "New Dimes May be Recalled: Coins Bear Initials of Designer, Held to be Violation of Law," *Mehl's Numismatic Monthly,* January 1917, p. 10.

Chapter 18: An Indecent Coin

1. See Robert R. Van Ryzin, "An Artist's Written Word: The Letters of Hermon A. MacNeil Bring His Brilliant Career in Sculpture to Life," *Coins,* July 1988, pp. 66, 68-72.
2. J.H. Cline, *Standing Liberty Quarters,* (Dayton, Ohio: By the Author, 1976), p. 29.
3. Ibid.
4. Ibid., p. 32.
5. U.S. Department of Treasury, *Annual Report of the Director of the Mint for the Fiscal Year Ending June 30 1916 Including Report on the Production of the Precious Metals During the Calendar Year 1915* (Washington, D.C.: Government Printing Office, 1916), p. 8.
6. Cline, p. 45.
7. "New Designs Trouble Mint: Cannot Make Satisfactory Dies for Dimes, Quarters and Half Dollars," *Mehl's Numismatic Monthly,* October 1916, p. 130. The press notice (dated Sept. 15) from

★★★

Philadelphia added that: "According to Dr. Albert A. Norris, chief clerk of the Philadelphia Mint, the die makers usually have trouble when designs are made by artists who are not familiar with the mechanical problems." The December issue of Mehl's monthly recorded that new dimes were at hand, with some 3 million having been coined in October 1916 at Philadelphia.

8. Cline, p. 45.

9. Ibid., p. 46.

10. Don Taxay, *The United States Mint and Coinage: An Illustrated History From 1776 to the Present* (New York: Arco Publishing Co. Inc., 1966), p. 349.

11. "Designs of New Quarters Subject to Minor Change," *Mehl's Numismatic Monthly*, March 1917, p. 47.

12. U.S. Congress, House. *Congressional Record*, 65th Congress, 1st sess., 25 June 1917, p. 4223.

13. Cline, p. 50.

14. *The Lloyd M. Higgins, M.D. Collection and Other Properties*, Jan. 28-30, 1988 (Wolfeboro, N.H.: Auctions by Bowers and Merena, 1988), p. 41.

15. "May Change Design of New Quarter Dollar," *The Numismatist*, March 1917, p. 111.

16. "Revised Design for U.S. 1917 Quarter Dollars," *The Numismatist*, November 1917, p. 481.

17. "Editorial: Miss Liberty Now in a Gown of Mail?" *The Numismatist*, November 1917, pp. 470-471.

Sidebars

1. "The Broken Sword on the New Peace Dollar," *The Numismatist*, February 1922, p. 101.

2. "Criticizes the Eagle on Quarter Dollar," *The Numismatist*, March 1925, p. 179.

3. J.H. Cline, *Standing Liberty Quarters* (Dayton, Ohio: By the Author, 1976), pp. 55-59.

Chapter 20: Seeing Double

Sidebars

1. "The New Dime," *Mehl's Numismatic Monthly*, January 1917, p. 9.

Chapter 21: A Nation's Dime

1. Don Taxay, *The US. Mint and Coinage: An Illustrated History From 1776 to the Present* (New York: Arco Publishing Co. Inc., 1966), p. 371.

2. Ibid., p. 375.

3. Cornelius Vermeule, *Numismatic Art in America: Aesthetics of the United States Coinage* (Cambridge, Mass: The Belknap Press of Harvard University Press, 1971), p. 208.

4. Ibid., pp. 208-209.

5. Interview with Dr. Selma Burke, 1993. Same for following quotations. See also, Robert R. Van Ryzin "Who Really Designed the Roosevelt Dime: Leading Black Sculptor Clings to Belief That Roosevelt Dime Design Hers, Not Sinnock's," *Numismatic News* 30 November 1993, p. 1.

★ ★ ★

6. "'Peace' is Truman's Plea at Dedication of Roosevelt Plaque," Washington, D.C. *Evening Star,* Sept. 25, 1945.
7. "John R. Sinnock, Coin Designer," *Numismatic Scrapbook Magazine,* March 1946, p. 261.
   Sidebars
1. "Stalin Initial Rumor Revived," *Numismatic Scrapbook Magazine,* March 1952, p. 298.
2. "He'll Find it There, All Right," *The Numismatist,* April 1926, p. 155.
3. Breen, p. 247.

Chapter 22: An Unsinkable Coin
1. Eric P. Newman and Kenneth E. Bressett, *The Fantastic 1804 Dollar* (Racine, Wis.: Whitman Publishing Co., 1962). The authors note that this story appeared in Ivan C. Michels, *The Current Gold and Silver Coins of All Nations,* Philadelphia, 1880, and in subsequent editions.
2 "With Editors and Advertisers," *The Numismatist,* November, 1899, p. 244.
3. "Will Remain Forever in Chicago," *The Numismatist,* February 1905, pp. 53-54.
4. "Counterfeits and Forgeries in Ancient and Modern Coins," *The Numismatist,* July 1937, p. 617.
5. "The 1804 Dollar Again," *The Numismatist,* March 1899, p. 56.
6. Ibid.

Chapter 23: A Pretend Indian
1. "The Indian Head Cent," *The Numismatist,* November 1931, p. 804.
2. Reprinted in "Not Sara Longacre on Indian Cent," *Numismatic Scrapbook Magazine,* March 1951, p. 197.
3. Ibid.
4. Ibid.
5. Ibid., p. 198.
6. Ibid.
7. Walter Breen, "More About Longacre's Indian Cent Model," *Numismatic Scrapbook Magazine,* April 1951, p. 297.
8. Ibid, p. 298.
9. Walter Breen, "Our $3 Coin Born to Placate the Gold Interests," *Coins,* August 1968, p. 28.
10. Rev. Lindsay B. Longacre, "Longacre's Indian Cent Design," *Numismatic Scrapbook Magazine,* November 1951, p. 1006.
11. Rick Snow, *Flying Eagle and Indian Head Cents* (Seahurst, Wash.: Eagle Eye, 1994), p. 8.
12. Ibid.

* * *

Bibliography

Books:

Berrey, Lester V. and Van Den Bark, Melvin. *The American Thesaurus of Slang.* 2nd ed. New York: Thomas Y. Crowell Co., 1953.

Betton, James L., ed. *Money Talks: A Numismatic Anthology Selected From Calcoin News.* California State Numismatic Association, 1970.

Bowers, Q. David. *The History of United States Coinage: As Illustrated by the Garrett Collection.* Los Angeles, Calif.: Bowers and Ruddy Galleries Inc., 1979.

Breen, Walter. *Walter Breen's Complete Encyclopedia of U.S. and Colonial Coins.* New York: F.C.I. Press, Doubleday, 1987.

Bridges, William. *Gathering of Animals: An Unconventional History of the New York Zoological Society.* New York: Harper and Row, 1974.

Cline, J.H. *Standing Liberty Quarters.* Dayton, Ohio: By the author, 1976.

Cohen, Annette R. and Druley, Ray M. *The Buffalo Nickel.* Arlington, Va.: Potomac Enterprises, 1979.

Crosby, Sylvester S. *The Early Coins of America.* Lawrence, Mass.: Quarterman Publications, reprint ed., 1983. Originally published by the author as *The Early Coins of America and the Laws Governing Their Issue.* Boston, 1875.

Davis, Norman C. *The Complete Book of United States Coin Collecting.* New York: Mcmillan, revised ed., 1976.

Dryfhout, John H. *The Work of Augustus Saint-Gaudens.* Hanover, N.H.: University Press of New England, 1982.

Evans, George G. *Illustrated History of the United States.* Philadelphia: George G. Evans, Publisher, new revised ed., 1888.

Julian, R.W. *Medals of the United States Mint: The First Century 1792‑1892.* El Cajon, Calif.: Token and Medal Society, 1977.

Knepper, Cathy D. *Dear Mrs. Roosevelt: Letters to Eleanor Roosevelt Through Depression and War.* DeCapo Press, 2006.

Kosoff, Abe. *Abe Kosoff Remembers… 50 Years of Numismatic Reflections.* New York: Sanford J. Durst Numismatic Publications, 1981.

Krakel, Dean. *End of the Trail: The Odyssey of a Statue.* Norman, Okla.: University of Oklahoma Press, 1973.

Lewis, Arthur H. *The Day They Shook the Plum Tree.* New York: Harcourt, Brace & World Inc., 1963.

Martin, Lee. *Coin Columns.* Anaheim, Calif.: Clarke Printing, 1966.

Newman, Eric P. and Bressett, Kenneth E. *The Fantastic 1804 Dollar.* Racine, Wis.: Whitman Publishing Co. 1962.

Pollock III, Andrew W. *United States Patterns and Related Issues.* Wolfeboro, N.H.: Bowers and Merena Galleries Inc., 1994.

Snow, Rick. *Flying Eagle and Indian Head Cents.* Seahurst, Wash.: Eagle Eye, 1994.

Taxay, Don. *The U.S. Mint and Coinage: An Illustrated History From 1776 to the Present.* New York: Arco Publishing Co. Inc., 1966.

Tharp, Louise Hall. *Saint-Gaudens and the Gilded Era.* Boston: Little, Brown and Co., 1969.

★ ★ ★

Van Ryzin, Robert R. *Crime of 1873: The Comstock Connection*, Iola, Wis.: Krause Publications, 2001.

Van Ryzin, Robert R. *Striking Impressions: A Visual Guide to Collecting U.S. Coins.* Iola, Wis.: Krause Publications, 1991.

Van Ryzin, Robert R. *Twisted Tails: Sifted Fact, Fantasy and Fiction from U.S. Coin History.* Iola, Wis.: Krause Publications, 1995.

Vermeule, Cornelius. *Numismatic Art in America: Aesthetics of the United States Coinage.* Cambridge, Mass.: The Belknap Press of Harvard University Press, 1971.

Yeoman, R.S. A *Guide Book of United States Coins*, Racine Wis.: Whitman Publishing, 1947

Journals, magazines, newspapers:

O'Leary, Paul M. "The Scene of the Crime of 1873 Revisited: A Note." *The Journal of Political Economy* 69 (August 1960): 288-392.

Various issues of *Coins, Coin World, The Century Illustrated Monthly, Esquire, Mehl's Numismatic Monthly, Numismatic News,* and *Numismatic Scrapbook Magazine.*

Weinstein, Allen. "Was There a 'Crime of 1873'?: The Case of the Demonetized Dollar." *The Journal of American History* 54 (September 1967): 307-326.

Government documents:

U.S. Congress, House. *Congressional Record*, 65th Congress, 1st sess., June 25, 1917, p. 4223.

U.S. Department of Treasury. *Annual Report of the Director of the Mint for the Fiscal Year Ended June 30, 1916* and also *Report on the Production of Precious Metals in the Calendar Year 1915.* Washington, D.C.: Government Printing Office, 1916.

U.S. Department of Treasury. *Twenty-Fourth Annual Report of the Director of the Mint to the Secretary of the Treasury for the Fiscal Year Ended June 30, 1896.* Washington, D.C.: Government Printing Office, 1897.

U.S. Department of Treasury. *Twenty-Second Annual Report of the Director of Mint to the Secretary of the Treasury for the Fiscal Year Ended June 30, 1894.* Washington, D.C.: Government Printing Office, 1894.

Auction catalogs:

The Lloyd M. Higgins, MD. Collection and Other Properties, Jan. 28-30, 1988. Wolfeboro, N.H.: Auctions by Bowers and Merena, 1988.

* ⭐ *

Made in the USA
Lexington, KY
05 January 2017